# Pop Idol™

## The official inside story

# The official inside story

## Siân Solanas

CARLTON BOOKS

Author's Acknowledgements

This book would have been impossible to write without the sterling work of Beck Eleven at FremantleMedia; the steely dedication of Lorna Russell and Gillian Holmes; and the withering wit of Mr Solanas.

Siân Solanas

This is a Carlton Book

First published in Great Britain in 2004 by

Carlton Books Ltd, 20 Mortimer Street, London W1T 3JW

Photographs by Brian J. Ritchie and Ken McKay

A catalogue record for this book available from the British Library.

ISBN 1 84442 876 1

Printed and bound in the UK by Butler and Tanner Ltd,

Frome and London

Project Editor: Lorna Russell

Art Director: Clare Baggaley

Designer: Sooky Choi

Jacket Designer: Alison Tutton

Production: Lisa Moore

The publishers would like to thank Hayley Chapman and Pat Smith at Granada Picture Desk for all their help.

# Contents

# Welcome Back

*Welcome back to Pop Idol – the return of the most successful talent show ever, beating even The Queen's Speech (probably) in TV ratings. Last time round, Will Young won the competition with a staggering 4.6 million votes – (53.1%) – beating his buddy Gareth Gates and becoming a number one pop sensation overnight.*

The National Grid called ITV to check advert break times before the final show, amid fears of a power cut from huge surges in electricity demands. Even Tamsin Outhwaite and Ricky Gervais were seen at the *Pop Idol* party that night. Here's what some people had to say about the last series:

'I loved it, it was mega!'
– Jimi Hendrix

'What a show! I never failed to set my VCR, momma!'
– Elvis Presley

'Pardon?' – J-Lo

With the debut release of Will Young's double A-side, 'Evergreen' / 'Anything Is Possible', records were broken for the biggest single ever with sales at 1.8 million. Gulp. Will Young occupied the top spot for three weeks, stepping down when Gareth Gates charted with his debut single, 'Unchained Melody'. Sir Gates shifted an amazing one million records in the first week and also became the second fastest-selling debut of all time. So, like, entering *Pop Idol* was worth it after all.

Now the *Pop Idol* monster is back, ready to craft and create the nation's next singing sensation. And the turnout is huge. Over 20,000 people have queued up this year, setting themselves up for unequalled praise or sheer ridicule by the now infamous judging panel.

And in case you've been on the moon this past year or so, shall we just run through who those judges are again? Go on.

## Nicki Chapman

Creative Director of 19 Entertainment working closely with Simon Fuller on future entertainment projects and programmes. Working in promotion and then management, she has worked with the top names in the crazy world of showbiz, including Annie Lennox, The Spice Girls, Phil Collins, S Club 7 and Charlotte Church. More recently she's overseen the careers of a certain Mr Will Young and a Mr Gareth Gates. She's also been seen on TV as a presenter of *The Morning Show*, *Escape to the Sun* and *City Hospital*.

Nicki lives in London, likes diving and shopping. But not at the same time.

## Simon Cowell

Millionaire record bigwig. Started a record label in the '80s that housed, amongst others, Sinitta. He has worked for BMG records looking after Five and Westlife, and the Teletubbies. In the last ten years, Cowell has achieved sales of over 90 million records, over 70 top 30 records and 34 number one singles. That's a lot. He helped to develop *Pop Idol* with pal Simon Fuller, who was responsible for The Spice Girls and Annie Lennox, to name but two.

Simon then went to show the US what high-waisted trousers he had for two series of *American Idol* and had Michael Aspel rifle through his memories with *This Is Your Life*. Simon is 42, lives in London and LA and has a lovely girlfriend called Terri.

## Neil Fox

Foxy is without doubt one of UK radio's most popular, most listened-to and most successful Superstar DJs ever. As well as his daily show for Capital FM in London, he is of course the nation's Chartmaster, having hosted the Sunday countdown, formerly the Pepsi Chart and now known as *HIT40UK*, for over a decade. He has won pretty much every award going, both here and internationally, and this put together with his incredible interviews over the years with the world's greatest singers and artists, has given him a truly awesome insight into the whole concept of X-factor… and more importantly, how to spot it!

Foxy has also hosted three ITV series over the last 18 months and has something pretty spectacular up his sleeve for after *Pop Idol*! He is married to Vicky, has two littleFoxcubs called Scarlet and Jack, and lives in London.

## Pete Waterman

A bigger music knowledge you will not find. Pete started DJing at clubs in the '60s, bringing R&B to his audience and then Motown. He worked in many aspects of the music business during the '70s, signing artists and discovering new bands. In 1984 he worked with Mike Stock and Matt Aitken and between them they have produced hits for Kylie Minogue, Steps, Sonia, Westlife and trillions more. Pete was awarded an Honorary Doctorate by Coventry University in 2001.

All in all, Pete's created much of the pop music culture we have today, sold billions of albums and is a very enthusiastic talker on all subjects, but trains and pop music are his favourites.

## Ant and Dec

And there's Ant and Dec, who have been busy with the top shows *I'm A Celebrity Get Me Out Of Here!*, and *Ant and Dec's Saturday Night Takeaway*. Since the first *Pop Idol*, they've won Best Entertainment Personality for the second year running, as well as a Special Recognition award at the National Television Awards. They are still only 27 and have great hair.

## Kate Thornton

Kate Thornton anchors the gruelling ITV2 coverage. She's come a long way from editing *Smash Hits*, having presented shows such as *The Brits*, *Holiday You Call The Shots* and *Top Of The Pops* to name but a few. Kate also writes for the *Sunday Times* and *Marie Claire* magazine and hosts shows for Radio 2. This year, she's been asked out at least three times by admiring *Pop Idol* series 2 contestants, and has had one marriage proposal. Thus far, she hasn't accepted any offers.

# Pop Idol 2

## What's different this time around?

Well, the contestants should all know what to expect – they've seen the judges on *Pop Idol I* and they know they're going to be in for a grilling. Off camera, Simon Cowell thinks they're a lot mouthier and he mulls over the contestants with Pete Waterman during lunch. They discuss the 'get rich quick' culture that inspires our would-be stars. 'They want it all, *now*,' says Simon, eating a forkful of rice. 'Hearing about dot com millionaires and Lottery winners doesn't help. They don't want to work for it at all.' Everyone is surprised at how under-rehearsed some of the contestants are.

Ant McPartlin thinks that the contestants are a lot cockier. 'When we talk to them afterwards,' he says, 'They don't look at me or Dec, they look straight at the camera. They're far more aware they're being filmed and they could be on TV.'

## Who wants to be famous?

Well, almost everyone. Fame is a thing that people want more than ever. It's an illusive beast – hard to get your hands on, at the best of times. Is *Pop Idol* the best route to take in order to find it? Twenty thousand people thought so, as they turned up for the auditions. What, we thought, does it smell of, this fame? So we asked a few people at random:

## What does fame smell of?

Nicola: 'Money.'
Danny: 'Ice cream.'
Polly: 'Ooh! I can't tell you!'
James: 'The inside of a night club.'
Suzanne: 'Roses.'
Darren: 'New shoes. Not trainers, though.'

Still not sure, really. All we know is people desperately want to be famous. They're not sure why, but they do.

The most famous people here are the judges. They are trying not to mention the X-factor too much, and are preferring to be more open. Fresh from LA, Simon Cowell is still telling everything like it is (ie he's being direct again), but he is more tolerant this year. A little more relaxed, one thinks. Nicki is as lovely as ever, but if someone gets her goat then she will talk back. Foxy is using his strange expressions and Pete is as barking as before, telling people originality in pop is no good thing. Pardon?

# Who wants to be a Pop Idol?

Quite a lot of people, it seems. And most of them probably don't have what it takes. The judges are quick to spot people who they think are too cocky – lots of people don't want to be given advice. Some of the contestants who've come back for more – having auditioned for *Pop Idol I* or *Popstars: The Rivals* – are the worst offenders. Carla Winters, who made the last 50 in the first series, won't be told she's not good enough. She just doesn't want to know and causes a right old rumpus. 'This stubbornness – well, it doth not a good Pop Idol make' (© Shakespeare, who was a big Eric Clapton fan).

It's a difficult job, and you have to work at it 24/7. And sometimes 25/7 if you've been travelling and 'gained' an hour. And you can't stop when you're had your number one trillion-selling album, you know. You've got to sound and look good. All the time! You're up against the best.

# Pros and cons of being a Pop Idol

| Pros | Cons |
|------|------|
| Fame | The tabloids like to take pics of you when you've had too much 'Tizer' |
| Cash to buy lots of things | All your pals needing a 'loan' |
| Gorgeous girl/boyfriends | Jordan following you around |
| Artistic recognition | Being recognised when you are buying toilet roll |
| Parties | Having to eat little bits of chicken on a stick all your life |

## Pop stars that...
### a) have seen voice coaches:
Geri Halliwell
Darius Danesh
Gareth Gates
Britney Spears
Kylie

### b) have stylists to help them dress better:
Everyone

### c) should sack their stylist:
Christina Aguilera
Dannii Minogue

# 2003

## Where contestants went wrong...

1. There were lots of bad Christina Aguilera types, wailing 'Beautiful'. Mariah Carey's 'Hero' was another song that was sung completely over the top, as was the Daniel Bedingfield ballad 'If You're Not The One'.

2. People started singing too high, and got into trouble as the notes got even higher.

3. Lack of preparation was a problem for some. Lots would forget the words to songs.

4. Some would answer 'not sure' or 'can't decide' when asked what they were going to sing.

5. Some were bad on purpose. 'But I was bad!' They'd shout afterwards. 'Put me through!'

6. Chewing gum, wearing shades, hands in pockets or not looking at the judges are deemed very poor indeed.

### Top songs

*Even the youngest entrants were singing these OAP 'classics'...*

**'Get Here'** – Brenda Russell (more recently Oleta Adams)

**'Lately'** – Stevie Wonder

**'Falling'** – Alicia Keys

**'Right Here Waiting'** – Richard Marx

**'Easy'** – The Commodores

# The Auditions
## London

*Over 13 million people watched the Pop Idol final in 2001. This year, the contestants know that even if – especially if – they are bad they're going to get on the telly and be famous. Even if it's for just a few seconds. The judges have to sit through more versions of timeless ballads than ever before, and meet more gimmicks than is frankly necessary.*

From thousands, the judges have to pick just 100 to go on to the next stage of auditions at the Criterion Theatre, London. It's a tough job, but exceedingly well paid, eh?

The atmosphere is as tense as a very tense thing. People know what to expect, everyone knows that Simon can be very nasty. Perhaps – tremble – even nastier than series one … ooh. But as much as some people are primed to argue back, some falter. There are tears everywhere. People have come from as far afield as Cornwall, just for a minute in front of the judges… There's a girl who has a law exam and might even be late for it if she has to hang around any longer. Darn! She misses it *and* she doesn't go through! Argh.

What's surprising is how many people have come back for more. Lots of *Pop Idol I* contestants are here, trying for another chance. They know they could be in for an even harder time, but they don't care. Their judgement is blurred by the promise of fame and infinite riches.

Carla Winters, the young lady from *Pop Idol I*, auditions again. She reportedly dated Rik Waller, and then went on to reveal her comely chest in the 'news' papers after she failed to make the final ten. She says of the experience, 'It gave me a profile for a little bit, the only regret I have is saying things live on TV.' For when the judges didn't like her performance, she exclaimed: 'I did fancy you but I don't any more, Simon!' Uh-oh.

Today, the judges are not impressed. 'If anything, I think your voice has got worse,' says Foxy. Oh dear, she's not happy and refuses to leave the audition room until Tony the bouncer escorts her out. 'If you were in Grovelling Idol,' says Simon, 'You'd be in the top ten.'

Nathalie and sister Anne-Marie cause a minor storm. When the judges 'offend' Nathalie, she tells her sister. At Anne-Marie's audition she has a go at them.

*Natalie and Ann-Marie: Drank some tequila.*

Then Nathalie joins her sister and they both rail against the judges. 'I think you're having a laugh,' says Simon. 'She's amazing!' says Anne-Marie of Nathalie. 'Well start a record label and sign her up then,' replies Mr Cowell. They attempt to sing in unison but get carried out by security. 'I could smell the tequila from here,' says Mr Cowell. So talent smells of… spirits?

Some people walk into the room and say they're the nation's greatest undiscovered talent, and then sing completely out of tune. At one point, Pete describes it all as 'boring' and even Simon says, 'We're not finding great singers' but this is what happens all the time at *Pop Idol*. In fact, Foxy says that he doesn't think the standard is down this

*Carla Winters: 'dated' Rik Waller.*

year at all. 'You can't always see that there is a Will Young at first,' he says during lunch break. 'It takes time for people to develop.'

'And sometimes it's the opposite,' adds Simon. 'With Rosie Ribbons, she was great at the first auditions, then she never really got back to that level.'

There are people who look like pop stars, people who dress to impress (and, er, fail)… and then there's Chris, who looks a bit like a vicar.

'Well, that's what you look like.' Simon Cowell is not impressed with the way that young Chris presents himself. But what a voice! 'You're a cracking singer,' says Pete. 'Probably one of the most accomplished singers I've seen walk into this competition.' Simon agrees, sort of. 'If you walked into my office,' he snarls, 'I'd say forget it, based on the way you look; but you can sing.' After a little debate about whether he's got any 'personality', Chris goes through to the next stage.
'
And then there's Daniel, who looks like a librarian. 'You will never in a billion years be

a pop star,' says Simon Cowell when he hears Daniel say he'll come back year after year until he makes it through. Daniel's version of 'Insatiable' by Darren Hayes is the squeakiest, faintest, most dreadful thing for a while. But it has a certain charm. Daniel really, truly, honestly believes that one day he will become a pop star. A bit like Warren…

Oh Warren, poor misguided charisma-free chap. He causes a hoo-ha with his version of 'Eye Of The Tiger'. He shouts out the song with as much passion as if he is singing a shopping list while someone is hacking at his leg. He has just taken a maths degree, and sings in a band at Uni. 'You entertained me, but in the wrong way,' says Nicki. 'I did enjoy your performance, but it's a million miles away from what we're looking for.' But Warren! You've become the nation's hero!

Andy is here and is a familiar face. He was in the boy band 3SL and is Lisa Scott-Lee's brother. He is shivering with fear. Come on, he should know how to stand in front of a crowd by now, but no – the judges can make pop stars tremble.

*But could you say anyone talked his way in? Tarek, a banker from London, sings 'Sex Bomb'. He was not taking a 'you're rubbish' for an answer and got through when he pleaded. 'I think you're stark raving bonkers,' said Pete. Pete!?*

## What you didn't see at the auditions – Part I

Simon tells Ant and Dec that when they did their first impression of him and Pete in *Pop Idol I*, he didn't have a clue who they were.

No one has asked for any special catering, although Nicki likes to go for the low-fat option at lunch (she says she can't cook to save her life, her mashed potato is always lumpy, food fans), and Pete likes to have a pudding, even though he says he's on a diet.

*Warren: he can't sing.*

The talent in Glasgow is very mixed this year, with the judges putting less people through than at London. There are some proper people here – girls like Michelle and boys like Kieran who are not skinny little pop things (they both got through! Yay!).

There's a lot of talk from the judges about 'personality' – they're forever telling people they haven't got any, even though they've only met them for five minutes. The judges are not interested in identikit pop stars – they cringe when they see girls who seem to have modelled themselves on Girls Aloud (!) or boys who think they're Michael Jackson. **They want sparkle.**

Kieran is the man that gets the judges going – but only by the sound of his voice. He wears glasses, is a little overweight – but at least he is not dressed as a banana. He sings 'Faith' and wows Pete and Nicki, who says, 'You really did deliver that song.' But there's Simon again: 'I have a problem. Shutting my eyes, you're very good; then I look at you.' 'I want to be a singer, I don't want to be a model,' says Kieran, justly peeved. Pete butts in: 'To get where you want to go you have to change your attitude. It's not about being a model, it's about being presentable on the front of a magazine.' He gets through, and he promises to get down to the gym. 'Don't let me down!' says Pete as he leaves.

There's a man who likes his football, who's 6' 3" and as bald as a coot. It's Scott, who is very relaxed about the audition: 'My friends put me up for it!' he says. He saunters in, sings well, and gets through. He tries to look cool about it all but you can tell he's excited.

Who pops up once more? Jonathan Campbell who, looking about three years old, got into the final 50 of the last *Pop Idol*. He has a slicked-back (or greasy) mop of blond fringe now, but is still as wee as ever. The judging panel aren't utterly convinced, but they say they'll give him another go in London. Just as long as he washes his hair, mind.

## What you didn't see at the auditions – Part 2

There are letters from the concerned parents of some contestants who didn't make it through.

**'Dear Simon, You saw our boy/girl _____, who auditioned _____ and we think he/she deserves another chance.' Etc. etc.**

Simon tells stories to the executive producers, which include phrases such as 'then we were in a room with 300 glamour girls.They call the line of seats outside the audition room 'death row'.

Contestants quietly sip from bottles of water, or chat nervously, knowing their time is soon 'up'. Oh yes. The day of reckoning, with the four judges of the apocalypse.

# Manchester

Mario entertains with 'Wheels On The Bus', in the holding room, and he's proved a big hit with fellow contestants. In the audition room, he implores the judges to let him through, but they are not taken with his novelty act and refuse (but see *What you didn't see at the auditions – Part III* for more). At one point Simon wants to call it 'Pop Idol-ish', because he's not sure they've found anyone amazing in the last day or so. Pete gets batey again, but this happens every day (usually mid-afternoon).

There's a person called David Graham who claims that he's played in front of 500,000 and has 130,000 letters from the public who are interested in him. Simon says he's lying – well, he does look a bit intense. Ashley, who is blind, does not go through and she is 'furious' afterwards; the judges telling her that her voice doesn't have an 'edge' makes her very hot under the collar. 'You will see me on your TV screens in two years' time,' she promises/warns.

Danny Tetley, and his unusual hair, returns. He doesn't inspire the judges, however, and they have a big chat with him. Nicki reckons he should be a backing singer, but he's not really listening. He's set his heart on solo stardom, y'see, and that could be his big mistake. 'He's made himself look like an idiot, coming here today,' says Pete as frankly as ever.

Pop Idols must have a dream. But many mistake dreams and delusions. Brendan first says he's 24. Then he says he's between 26 and 36 ('just under Nicki's age'). **He finally admits to being 42.** He looks like an eighties pop star (ie in his eighties, ha ha) and his hair has been salvaged from a dying cat, He sings a medley (mostly Pete's hits) and has as much musical talent as a doorknob. Bless him, er, probably, although the papers are full of his antics as a male 'escort' the next week. Groo.

Nicola Gates turns up again this year, and decides she wants to be known as Nicola J, because she doesn't want to be in her brother's shadow. 'The last year and a half has been spent gaining more experience, I think I've grown up a lot,' she says before her audition. 'I'm a little nervous, there's some very stunning people here, but I'm sure I can sing.' She wears a white suit with the one-leg-tucked-in hip-hop look. But no! The judges are hypercritical.

'When we saw you before,' says Simon, 'You were naïve, and you looked like you were enjoying it. Today it looked like an effort. You look overstyled.' After a debate, she gets through, although Simon says it's because she's Gareth's sister. Foxy is livid.

'That's b*******!' he says to Simon, who shrugs. Well, he does have to keep Mr Gates happy… doesn't he?

The last person in the whole auditions is Suzanne, the very last person last time was… Will Young.

Suzanne is understandably nervous, but does a great audition. 'You're like a ray of sunshine' says Nicki, and she goes through to London… Hoorah.

*Nicola 'J': 'Overstyled'.*

# What you didn't see at the auditions – Part 3

The judges are unsure about Mario – well, actually they think he's rubbish – but he won't let up. Simon decides he should go into Manchester city centre, find three people who would buy his recording of 'Wheels On The Bus' and bring them back. Half an hour later… he does! Three sheepish but quite convinced (ie mad) young ladies will admit to wanting to spend £4 on this 'art'. The judges tell him he can't sing. 'Can everyone sing before they become a pop star?' he asks, desperately. 'Yes!' they reply, in unison.

One girl, Marie, arrives in Manchester and is shocked to see other people there, 'I thought I'd be the only one auditioning today!' she says.

## The rest of the worst

The Cheeky Girls effect: will these people become famous because they are so bad?

*Bananaman* – Gary sings 'I've Got You Under My Skin'. The judges are not amused.

*Suleman* – He believes he can fly, while moving his head like a pigeon when it walks.

*Andrew as Elvis* – 'Simon wasn't loving me very much.' That's because you told him to shut up, Andrew.

*Marie Louise* – Fails to start her song and then storms out.

*Hayley* – Sang Britney like a wounded lamb, with a funny throat.

*Fiona* – Wore a bra. Sounded dreadful.

*Pejman* – Sings 'Beautiful' by Christina Aguilera, and it isn't. Simon tells him to pray for a miracle.

*Camillas* – Pete: 'What do you think about that performance?' Camillas: 'It needs a bit of work.' Nicki: 'Understatement of the year.'

*Rachel* – She sings Dido. 'If you heard that version in a car you'd crash,' says Simon.

*Stalker Daniel* – Knows everything about the judges, looks like a toilet brush in a gold suit, sings funny, convinced he's a star.

*Chris* – Another maths student (see Warren) who thinks he might get through by singing 'Great Balls Of Fire'. Simon tells him his chances are a million to one.

## You think we were joking about the smell of fame?

Think again, youngsters, because we weren't. Pop Idol has created a fragrance, and it can help you smell like a pop star; whether you look like one, sing like one, or have no interest in being one whatsoever.

### Goat Idol

A few auditionees had no control over their voices, or mouths, or whatever it might be, because many warbled their way through the classics. 'You should be on Goat Idol,' said Foxy to one. 'If you make that show I'll come back for it,' she replied. A whole new genre of music is born…

## So you think you can sing?

Many people think they can belt out a wonderful tune, and deserve pop stardom like they deserve their legs. But they can't sing. They have no idea. They are tuneless. Does this happen when *you* open your mouth?
Glass shatters?
Dogs howl?
Friends flee for cover?
Old people suddenly feel a bit peaky?
Whole towns collapse?
Believe it or not (and most *Pop Idol* contestants won't), if you answered yes to most of these, the likelihood is that you can't sing.

### 'This is the last show in which the judges decide who stays and who goes...' Ant McPartlin

The evening before the auditions begin, the 100 wannabes have all checked in at the St Giles Hotel, central London. The place is a flurry of colour, the chatter and laughter are loud; they have taken over the building. Their first task is to stand before the camera and complete the phrase, 'I want to be a Pop Idol because…' Little do they know that the judges are sitting in the next room, watching. And, goodness me, do those judges make some comments.

**Foxy:** 'He'd charm the knickers off a nun.'
**Pete:** 'He looks like an advert for a Clearasil commercial.'
**Nicki:** 'Ooh, no life in those eyes.'
**Simon:** 'The only problem is, Demis Roussos [plumpy '70s Greek singer] is not a good role model.'

The judges are a bit disappointed. They find a lot of the contestants are very earnest (quite a few thank God for their talent, hmm), there's not much spark and they are worried that no one is showing their personality.

*Says Nicki: 'They had two weeks to think of something, and that's what they've come up with. It's disappointing. There were only four people who were good there.'*
*'It's hard to think one of those will be the Pop Idol,' says Foxy.*
*'Ah, but I think we've seen the winner,' says Simon, all mysterious like.*

Immediately after, the judges hold a conference with the final 100. This is time for The Truth. Pete reckons they're not going to get millions of viewers on a Saturday night unless they buck their ideas up. Watch out, contestants.

'I've just sat through "Why I want to be a Pop Idol,"' Simon tells the crowd, 'And it was possibly the most boring hour and a half of my life. You have to start showing your true personalities. What we've proved is that the prize is worth winning, unlike any other TV competition.'

When the judges ask if anyone's got any questions, young Eddie pipes up, wondering whether he'll have to sing any of those 'crap' cover versions. Foxy tells him Elvis, Sinatra and Diana Ross never wrote their own songs. Simon says, 'Anyone who can write a better song than "Evergreen", I'll write them a cheque for half a million,' but he commends Eddie for speaking up.

Wesu tells the panel his wife is due to give birth in the next couple of days – will he be out of the competition if he has to rush back for the great event? Yes! say the judges. Wesu is understandably upset by this, but vows to give the competition his all.

## What you didn't see at the conference...

*The judges do admit, before they talk to the contestants, that George Michael wrote a great song – 'Careless Whisper' – when he was 17, on a bus! And they note that Lennon and McCartney were writing top tunes when they were still at Art College. Thus, someone in the room might be writing corking pop tunes, and they mustn't always be down on people who want to be involved in the songwriting process. However, better to have a wonderful tune that gets to number one and sells billions, than a half-written load of tripe that has artistic 'integrity' but no catchy chorus, eh? Eh?*

# Day One

### 'The competition's getting tougher, and that shows' Pete Waterman

The contestants are *so* nervous. Perhaps last night's chat didn't help much, 'cos they're a-quakin' in their boots. Today, 100 will shrink down to 75, and tomorrow, 75 become 50 as the battle gets tough.

'At the first auditions,' says Dec, 'They said, "If I get through to the last 100, then I'll be fine; they haven't seen the real me yet." And now that they're here they say, "I just want to get through this stage, *then* they'll see the real me."'

But there have been some transformations. Eddie says he's lost two stone. Paula Jade has dyed her hair back to blonde. Kieran and Craig have also lost weight. *Pop Idol* fever has got to some and they are dedicated; they *want* that dream so badly. First off, everyone sings one song solo.

Chris, previously called a 'vicar' in his first audition, has lost the glasses, and a couple of pounds in weight, and sings with a voice that lights up the auditorium. Pete loves him, although Simon is not impressed this time. Craig – who was so nervous beforehand (and whom the judges said will make the top ten), sings 'She Bangs' by Ricky Martin and swivels his hips around. Simon thinks he chose the wrong song. Foxy tells mouthy Tarek that his ego outweighs his talent. He might have a point.

Of the girls, Rebecca absolutely wows the judges, Foxy's still swooning (she's the 'naughty and nice' girl) and Simon's looking immensely pleased. Rachel, the bingo caller, wears luminous colours so bright she looks like a fluorescent parrot. The judges love her bubbly personality, but reckon she's still got a lot to learn as a singer. Nicola J, Gareth Gates' sister, sings well but looks nervous. Pete tells her she's 'walking in giant

footsteps'. She refuses to talk to Ant and Dec after her song, and is very upset. It's extra hard for her, because everyone knows who she is and she can't be just 'Nicola'.

It must be noted, the judges really do remember everyone – well, almost everyone – and note how each performance differs and what the contestant's strengths and weaknesses are. When they say, 'In Manchester I thought you were very good at belly-dancing', they really do *remember*. Which is wonderful when you consider how they could be thinking about what to have for their tea or how many trillions they've earned in the past hour etc.

At the end of this first day, decisions are made. The contestants are sent to sit in rooms: yes, no and maybe. Phrases like 'walking on eggshells', 'walking on thin ice', 'it could be the end of the road' are bandied about like nobody's business. The maybes get through, but are told they must work hard tomorrow. Simon also adds that Will and Darius were maybes last year... so there's hope yet.

Nicola J doesn't get through. 'I think it was my nerves,' she says. 'I tried my best, but I didn't have a clue what to expect...' Off screen, the judges are thoughtful. 'It wasn't an easy decision,' says Simon. 'If we'd kept her in it would have been patronising.' 'We had to go on who *she* is,' says Nicki, 'irrespective of who her brother is. Her audition wasn't good enough.' Nicki goes to chat with her before she leaves, because she knows she's upset.

## Day Two

### 'That's what I call a "three A" performance: awful, awful, awful' Simon Cowell

Last night the task was to learn a song in a night, and everyone gets into groups of three and rehearses. Some stay up for most of the night, going through the moves and learning the words and some… don't.

And let's be honest, this part of the auditions *really* shows up the, er, weaker performers. Some of the groups wobble around each other, like shortsighted fish in a bowl, forgetting the words, the tune, and to stop gargling in the background when someone else is trying to sing. And then… others shine. Rebecca's group are praised for being a tight unit. Kim and Michelle's group sing 'Baby Love' to rapturous applause from the boys, who watch the show from the auditorium. Kieran's group get told there's *one* good performer in the trio – and Simon won't say *who*… Andy Scott Lee is told he's not the best singer here, Wesu (hoorah! He's still here 'cos his wife has not given birth yet…) is told he's not as good as he thinks he is. Oh you judges! You can be so cruel sometimes.

## What you didn't see…

*Reports had it that Nicola Gates was going to bring her brother along to the auditions, then thought better of it. Yes, it was wise not to…*

*At the Criterion, the girls watch the boys perform and vice versa. Whenever Simon makes an honest remark, the girls boo him.*

*In a marked difference to the first Pop Idol, the girls are all wearing micro minis, high heels and tiny tops. 'It's the Top Shop Pop School!' says Foxy. 'Or the Atomic Kitten School Of Auditions,' counters Simon.*

The judges have to make their final decision in the Criterion auditorium, as the contestants wait upstairs in the bar area. *No one* is allowed to sit in on selection process.

Many contestants have been too nervous to eat properly today, and sit and chat with newfound friends. Nobody wants to think of those terrifying judges, making their terrifying pronouncements… there's a bit of a group sing-song, but some sit outside in the corridor, needing a bit of peace. Scott is justly nervous, having been called 'awful' by Simon. Yiannis joins him, and he too is afraid, very afraid.

'I think they're nastier than they were,' says Scott of the fearsome four. 'But I've got used to it.' 'I think they were a lot nastier to the girls today,' says Yiannis. They both look like they're sitting outside the headmaster's office…

An hour or so later and the contestants are arranged in groups of five. Each group is told whether they will or won't go through to the next stage of auditions at Teddington studios. The people who leave are clearly sad, but resolute. Grace – she of the amazing tonsils – says we'll be seeing her sometime in the future, not to worry. Being told she was 'too cool for school' wasn't exactly what she wanted to hear. 'I was only being myself…' she says.

But for those who are through to Teddington, the stakes are raised. And it's simply *more* terrifying, because their fate is in your hands.

# Meet the Judges

## Nicki Chapman

### If this is reality TV, how real is it?

It's real in that we ask people to do something that's very difficult, very demanding, quite stressful and you've really got to want to do it to go forward for it, but it's an entertainment show.

### Have you changed your approach as a judge?

Perhaps I'm a little tougher because I want better reactions and better performances this year.

### Have you lost your rag at all?

I flew off the handle at Tarek for interrupting me all the time, and there have been a couple of instances where people have verbally attacked Simon and Pete saying, 'The record industry is abusing people!' and I went for them. You don't need people who are ill-informed making statements like that.

### What will the winner have to face?

Everyone will compare them with Will and Gareth, because of their success. On the other side they've been able to watch it and see what happens to their lives, so although you can't prepare for it, you will have felt like you've witnessed it a little bit.

### Was it difficult for Nicola Gates in entering the competition?

I think she had a disadvantage, I think the competition was too big for her, that's the truth. I think she came in on a negative, she felt everything in a very negative way and I don't think she helped herself – she was very aware of who she was, and whose sister she was. She did a better audition the first time. I think nerves got to her.

### Are you envious of Simon's bouncer?

Ha ha! I don't need a bouncer, I don't think people would take a pop at me. It was wise we had one for Simon. He looks after all of us, but 99.99999% of his time is with Simon.

### When will we see Jordan popping her head round the [hotel] door?

Hopefully we won't, because she doesn't sing. She has other assets. She hasn't got her oar in as far as *Pop Idol II* is concerned, only regarding an ex-contestant of *Pop Idol*, and I think she's had lots to say about that. She might say '*I love Tarek now! He's the one!*' You never know.

# Simon Cowell

### What have you taken from the American Idol experience?

I think most of the feedback I had in America was that I was being honest with the kids. You have to say what's on your mind and not become a caricature of yourself. And you have to ignore the hype and do what you're paid to do, which is to offer them your experience.

### What's the standard here like?

It's safe, but it's inevitable on the second series that the people who watched the first show play cautious, they don't take risks, and that sometimes goes in your favour and many times it goes against you. Now they know what is at stake if they win, the desire is obviously stronger. I saw it in America on the second series and I'm seeing it here. This is no longer just a laugh, people really want to win this.

### Why do people come back for more, year after year?

I think in some cases they're just nuts coming back a second time. It's funny, most of the people who come back the second time are much more egotistical.

### Do people want fame more than they did a few years back?

Yeah. I think we live in a fame epidemic. Everyone wants be famous, that's why shows like *Big Brother* get so many applicants. They're not doing it to win the money, they're doing it to become famous.

### How do Gareth, Will and Darius cope with fame?

You'd have to ask them. Probably the one who's enjoying it more than anyone else is Darius. Gareth – because of his age – is going through that phase of discovering all the things that eighteen-year-olds discover. Good luck to him… and Will looks a lot happier with his fame this year.

### Have you ever told anyone to become a plumber… and they did?

I think most people, when we tell them to forget it, don't take any notice of us.

### One imagines you sit there and create the perfect Pop Idol before you go on screen: 'We'll have J-Lo's bum, Gareth Gates' eyes…'

I think if you had described to me in advance of last year's competition, who would have won and what he sung in his first audition… and that the runner-up is a guy who can't even talk because he has a stammer, I wouldn't have thought that would happen, but that's the fun of the show.

### Has the pop world changed since Pop Idol I?

Yes. At the moment, in my opinion, it's a complete and utter mess, totally. The worst I've ever known it. *Pop Idol* gives kids a better chance than they would normally have, I don't think Will and Gareth would have got recording deals without it.

# Neil Fox

### Is there a certain type of person at the auditions this year?

There's not a certain type, although there are so many more this time that have seen what series one did for some of the contestants and are definitely thinking that this is the easy road to a quick fifteen minutes of fame! We sussed out the time-wasters and no-hopers pretty quickly and sent them off to *Big Brother*. Next we got rid of the dull and the bland and sent them to *Fame Academy*, and the rest of the Good, Bad and Ugly we kept for ourselves!

### Can tell from this stage who is going to do well?

You can get an indication at this stage, but what's easy at this stage is who's going to be a pain. We've noticed a few people – half a dozen – if they make it through any further they will be hard work, because they're full of attitude – too smug, too cocky and not willing to learn or take advice.

### People look petrified today...

I know and I can totally understand why. This quite simply is one of the most important days of their lives. You never get a second chance to make a first impression and so the pressure's really on. But that is what this industry is all about and something that our winner is going to learn to cope with. It is not enough to just be a great singer. You have to be a great performer and live with the nerves, or this is not the industry for you. Simple.

### How has your job changed playing records?

The music business is a very competitive one to work in and so is radio. It is a multi-billion pound industry and therefore it is more important than ever that as I become bigger and more successful, I play the records that I know my audience wants me to play while at the same time bring new music to their ears that I believe they are going to love. We are in a great period though at the moment for some awesome pop music (in its widest sense).

### You own a helicopter???

I really love flying and have held my chopper licence for eleven years. It is such a wonderful freedom, being up in the blue on a sunny day looking down on the world, but I do use it for business a lot and lease it out to help pay the bills. It's not as flash as it sounds but I am totally addicted! People ask if that means I am very wealthy, but I can always answer them that regardless of any material goods, I am a very rich man… I have a wonderful wife, two beautiful healthy kids and am extremely happy. Everything else is just a bonus.

### Did you enjoy the pizza in the Pop Idol Pizza Hut commercial?

I love pizza, who doesn't? It's gorgeous. But by the time we'd finished filming I think if any of us had been offered any pizza it was not going to be gratefully received. In the beginning we thought, 'Ahh! Great!' But by the end of the day we were pleading for them to stop bringing us any more!

# Pete Waterman

### What should the kids learn from auditioning for Pop Idol II?

That we are not *Big Brother*. We're not looking for just 'characters'.

### Do you think your honesty is ever cruel?

Yeah, you're a winner or loser, that's life. The natural selection that Darwin talked about.

### Do you regret what you said to Nicola Gates?

What did I say?

### That 'She's following giant footsteps…'

Well, she is. When is that an outrageous statement? Well, people say to my sons, 'You'll never be as good as your dad.' Is that not blunt? I hope they're wrong, but at this stage in time they've got a long way to go to catch up with their dad.

### What do you think the level of talent was like this year?

I think it's very much the same as last year, in truth. I keep hearing people make assumptions, but at this time last year nobody knew that Will was going to win; nobody knew he existed. He was put through 'cos we were short of boys. I'm hoping I could be pleasantly surprised that somebody pops up from this competition.

### Are there any people you've got your eye on?

I don't do that, but Simon has. If the guy that Simon has got his eye on wins, I'm sad. If you can spot it at this stage, before the live shows, if that's as good as it gets, then maybe it's time that I went and made classical albums.

### Simon thrives on having his favourites.

It's the way he works but it's not the way that I work. I want to be turned on my head, I want to hate someone then love 'em.

### Is this very different from Popstars: The Rivals?

Certainly, it's not the same sort of show. I carried that show on my own, this time it's a team, it's what it's all about. It's like one big family where everybody works together, we criticise each other, we know when it works and when it doesn't – and when that happens we try to make it work. I believe that's why we're successful and other shows like this *don't* work.

### What makes people want to be famous? Twenty thousand people applied this year.

Dunno. I know why I wanted to be famous, I didn't want to work down a coal mine, I wanted to be a millionaire. Ha ha!

### Do people ever come up to you in the street and say you were too cruel to the contestants?

The opposite, absolutely the opposite. The one thing they say to me – and it's interesting that suddenly I've got the baddy tag – is that I'm truthful, and I say things 'cos I feel them. I offer criticism.

### Why do some contestants come back for more, year after year?

They don't believe you in the first place.

### Can people get better?

I think that would stop everybody entering these competitions, wouldn't it?
Highly unlikely, but I'm not going to say it's impossible.

### Are you really looking for the next Mrs Waterman?

No. This is Simon's joke, isn't it? For some unknown reason he does love to have a go at me. Listen, it's great for TV, I've known him long enough not to get offended by it and as long as it's only Simon ribbing me I don't have a problem with it. If everybody starts, I might have.

# Pop Idol So Far

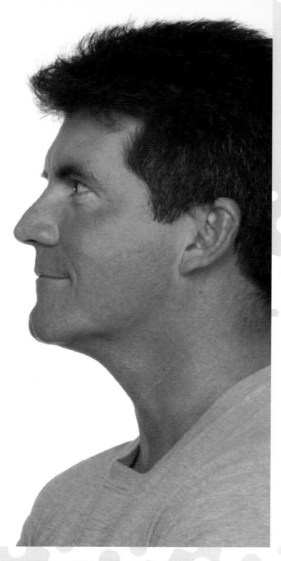

### Overheard conversation no 1 (Backstage tittle tattle no 1)

Pete has a bet with Simon that R Kelly has sold more than 800,000 copies of his single 'Ignition'. The bet is £1,000 cash. Simon rings his PA to check sales. Sales are less than 800,000. To date, Pete still hasn't given Simon the money.

### Overheard conversation no 2 (Backstage tittle tattle no 2)

Ant and Dec part-own a greyhound called Angel Of The North. Day three of the Manchester auditions, it's running in a race in Oxford. The production team bet over £100 on it to win. Simon puts a bet on the favourite and wins. 'I'll take my winnings and buy a greyhound, and get the best greyhound trainer in the world. Then I'll make it run in all the races against yours, and it will always beat you. Ha ha!' Simon is a cruel, cruel man.

# WHAT THEY SAID...

### Nicki's judgements are not always kind. Here are her comments on bad singing:

'Too nasal.'

'Wasn't the strongest of voices.'

'Too bland.'

'When you sing, do you hear pain?'

Ant and Dec to Pop Idol contestant: 'Do you sing a lot?'

Contestant: 'Not much.'

### Simon's put downs:

'You typify the problem in this country. Because of these competitions, people who have above-average talent believe they can be superstars.'

Contestant: 'How can I improve my voice?'

Simon: 'Pray for a miracle.'

'You are one above Ant and Dec.' [When they were PJ and Duncan.]

'People said I turned on Rik Waller because he was fat. I didn't like him 'cos he was a ____.' [You make up your own mind, readers, on Simon's choice of noun. NB It starts with a 'p'.]

'You are the musical equivalent of Valium.'

'We are looking for the equivalent of Gordon Ramsay, you are a Happy Eater.'

'I've got a headache, I'm tired and I'm getting emotional.'

'That is, I think, the most boring song I've heard in any Pop Idol audition.'

'You are not Manchester United, you are Dagenham.'

### Dr Fox is a man who likes to use very intricate comparisons when describing the contestants' talent. Our top five Foxy moments from the main auditions this year are, in ascending order:

5. 'You work in the perfume department. It's the packaging, all I could smell was "Tramp's".'

4. 'Jamie, you look good; you've got good balls. Er…' *Rest of judges groan at Foxy's slip, as he hides under the table.*

3. 'It's like telling Sven that you can't score a goal in the cup final.'

2. 'You're a travel agent? British Airways or EasyJet? You're not my world's favourite airline.'

1. 'You remind me of a chocolate éclair stuffed full of fresh cream, you are naughty and you are nice.'

### They'll say anything to be a Pop Idol...

'I want to help people, they can chill out, sort out their problems listening to me.'

### One contestant... who didn't make it to the auditions...

Was *Pop Idol* winner Will Young. He filled out an application form for the new series and put music as his interest but Nicki Chapman said his form was spotted because he used his correct address.

## A Glossary of Terms

### Judge-speak:

*Ghastly*

*Worst audition I've ever seen*

*You're crap!*

*I don't know what to say...*

*I can't make my mind up...*

*Is this a joke?*

*You find me someone who sings as badly as you and I'll put you through*

### The Real World:

*You could have done a bit better*

*Actually, I've seen worse*

*You'll probably become a novelty act and sell loads*

*I want my lunch*

*I need a toilet break*

*I'm not being paid enough*

*Just don't ask me to sing*

# Fifty become...Ten
# Heat 1

At Teddington Studios on a fresh autumn morning, the first group of ten from the final 50 are warming up the old vocal chords. This year, the vocal instructors are Ce Ce and John, who have worked with S Club, Will and Gareth and trillions more. Everyone has only 64 seconds to complete a verse and chorus, which they will sing to the judges, but they will be voted for by you, the viewers. Some songs have to be edited, some song choices changed, and a lot of work needs to be put in. Ce Ce makes everyone sing with a water bottle as if it were a microphone, so they get used to holding something.

On Tuesday, the atmosphere is very chilled. Contestants who aren't singing lounge around on beanbags, using the Magic 8 Ball toy to predict their future. 'I asked it whether I would get very far,' says Ema, dressed in fuchsia pink, 'and it said *I Doubt It.*'

But by the end of Tuesday Ce Ce is very pleased with the amount of work the ten have put in and the giant leaps they've made.

Today, the people of the press come down to watch the contestants sing their songs. Everyone's wondering what they will be like. Not to worry though, they are – on first appearance – a mild bunch. When Kate Thornton asks who they rate, most say Chris. He has already achieved a grand transformation, going from 'vicar' in the first audition to the 'Riffmeister' this week. For Chris is best known for the way he can ad-lib during a song, and include more notes in one single phrase than the finest gospel singers.

Michelle is name-checked too, for her 'mazin' pipes, but we shall see...

This ten are *very* well behaved. They've been going to bed early each night, all intent on doing their best. Everyone is taking it very seriously, which is good, but also means they're making themselves more anxious about their one chance to get into the final ten. This group have got nerves. Millions of them.

On the night, they are swamped with fear. Each of the ten thinks their group is especially strong, and they know they've got to do better than their best. The papers haven't helped – they're still printing stories about the public voting Michelle as *Pop Idol* 'winner' even though this first group of ten haven't performed yet, let alone the other 40 waiting for subsequent shows. This has piled the pressure on Michelle and not helped any of the others, who are so nervous they can hardly speak.

The contestants, who've had their confidence bolstered by Ce Ce and John, now have to face the judges. Pete Waterman says before the show, 'If they come across as unconfident, then they're gone.'

Oh no.

## The judges' verdict:

Simon Cowell tells Ema she is 'bland'. He blasts Jason for choosing the 'worst possible' song for his voice. He warns Rebecca that she isn't good enough for the competition. He tells Jade she is 'good-ish' etc. etc. All of them are in floods of tears afterwards. The others – including Ant and Dec – rally round to support their new chums. Eddie – who used to sport a very short 'n' tough haircut – is in tears too, and gurgles about how he's going to get the mick taken out of him by his mates… But when Michelle gets good news and is told by Simon that he wants her in the top ten… *she* starts crying! After the phone votes, and much nail-biting, our emotional contestants are told the results.

5th Eddie – 7.4%
4th Rebecca – 9.8%
3rd Jason – 17.4%
**2nd Chris – 19.3%**
**1st Michelle – 31.4%**

Cue more tears from Michelle and Chris *and* all the others who – after an intensive week and so much build-up – are simply shattered. 'So close, but so far away!' sniffs Jason, who can *not* be cheered up. Chris and Michelle say they simply can't believe it, whilst blubbing into their hankies. They've now got four weeks to prepare for the gruelling final ten shows…

# What you didn't see…

The judges ribbing Simon about being an hour late for filming – they say that he switches his mobile off so nobody can get hold of him.

Chris is level-headed when the press tip him this week. 'It did give me a bit of confidence when the press said I was their favourite, but it didn't last long because after they'd heard us sing, they said their favourites had changed.'

The ITV2 team brought in house plants to brighten the set up on Tuesday.

**Jason** – 22, Derby
**'Everything I Do'** (Bryan Adams)
Was at the local bus stop last week when a mob of girls ran to him and wanted to steal his cap. He had to run away.

**Ema** – 19, Preston
**'Hero'** (Mariah Carey)
Holds Anne Summers parties, selling their 'adult' range of toys and underwear. Saucy.

**Rebecca** – 23, London
**'Stop'** (Sam Brown)
Has sung backing vocals for American Idol winner Kelly Clarkson, on Top Of The Pops.

**Jade** – 16, Sheffield
**'I Wanna Dance With Somebody'** (Whitney Houston)
Once killed her older sister's goldfish; she still hasn't admitted this to her sister…

**Chris** – 18, West Sussex
**'End of the Road'** (Boys II Men)
Has grade eight in saxophone and singing.

**Michelle** – 23, Glasgow
**'Don't be a Stranger'** (Dina Caroll)
Was on a flight to London and the cabin crew told everyone over the tannoy that the girl from Pop Idol was on board.

**Tim** – 19, Chester
**'Just the Way You Are'** (Billy Joel)
The 'quiet one'. He comes from Zambia and was not, as rumour had it, part of an African tribe. Very good at table football.

**Helen** – 24, Surrey
**'Promise Me'** (Beverly Craven)
Tried to play Jade at table football and was completely thrashed.

**Eddie** – 27, Staffordshire
**'Still'** (Lionel Richie)
Has a twisted pelvis and can't move around properly on the day – he was laid up for two weeks when it first happened.

**Darja Schabad** – 20, London
**'Underneath Your Clothes'** (Shakira)
Speaks four languages.

# Fifty become...Ten

# Heat 2

*'I'd rather be a pop idol but if someone offered me a place in the Royal Family I wouldn't say no...'*
*Max on the endless comparisons between him and Prince William*

This week, *Pop Idol* fever is actually that – Jodie has an ear and throat infection, Adam's got flu, and the others are petrified they might get the lurgy and not be able to sing on Saturday night. Monday night after the first day's rehearsals they're all back in the hotel, towels on their head, breathing in the vapours of Friar's Balsam. Let's hope it works.

Despite the germs, this week's ten are determined. *Everyone* wants to go through, and they're giving it their all. It's a fair group – no one thinks anyone else has too much of an advantage – unlike last week when Michelle and Chris were tipped in the papers. Firstly, the group loosen up and sing together. The boys do a punk version of 'Lean On Me' and the girls a reggae version. Then everyone takes it in turns to go through their choice of song, which is sometimes changed if it's not showcasing their vocal talents enough. By Tuesday, all ten (except poor Jodie, who's only just joined them) are getting to grips with their performance and have to sing in front of the others.

The vocal coaches felt last week's ten did not live up to their promise. Nerves got them, and nerves mustn't. Oh no. Ce Ce explains that the worst-case scenario is that they're appearing on TV in front of the cream of bigwig record company people, scouring the programme for talent. If they're confident, but don't get through to the final ten, the very least they'll have is swanky meetings with excited record company types. 'I don't want to hear any negatives about you. You must be super positive,' adds John.

Then they both tell the contestants to sing whenever they're not doing anything, 'Just go and find a corner and practise.'

The studio is alive with the sound of music.

But singing is not just physical; it's emotional. A lot of feelings come to the surface when you're belting out a tune. Ce Ce explains, 'Singing is a vulnerable thing. I ask the contestants to tell me about themselves, what they've experienced, it helps them perform... someone started crying today.'

That person is Susanne, who is perhaps the most nervous and least confident of all the 50. She has a unique voice, she's good-looking and a lovely girl, but she's in tatters whenever she has to face an audience. Come on Susanne! Your public needs you!

By the time Simon arrives on Wednesday for the judges' comments – again, a little later than the other three members of the esteemed panel – the contestants have no idea if they will conquer their stage fright. It's all so *tricky* once you get up on that *Pop Idol* platform... 'People are voting for personalities, not voice, so it's still a bit of a soap opera' – Foxy is pondering the public vote. They think this week is a tough one to fathom – there are 'four good people' according to Nicki Chapman, but who might bottle it when it comes to their turn?

Ant and Dec are in a chirpy mood. They spent some of Tuesday texting ITV2 with things like 'Ant and Dec are *sooooo* fit!' and seeing their words broadcast over Kate

Thornton's show. Little chimps. They're wondering how many more people will be crying on their shoulders this week – they were most surprised by Eddie's tears, seeing as he's a big lad an' all.

## The judges' verdict

The big night arrives… and the judges hand out their verdicts. They are concerned many contestants are losing their individuality at this stage of the competition. Simon tells Bianca – who's ditched her once-trademark specs – exactly that. Foxy tells Max he's confused by what he's wearing (pink tie over tank top, mmmmm). 'Cabaret!' says Simon to Kelly-Marie. 'Next!' thinks Pete when Adam finishes. 'Stars In Their Eyes!' Simon tells Wesu.

But Simon does reserve praise for Susanne, Brian and Kirsty.

'Rubbish!' is what Bianca calls the judges' comments straight after she performs, and yus indeed, she is right – they're experts in their field, but they are NOT ALLOWED TO VOTE because they are NOT THE PUBLIC. Hoorah.

Results come through; it's been *very* close since the phone lines were opened, with the top four switching place *minute by minute*. Nail-bitingly, these are the final scores, Brucey. *

*5th Adam – 9.4%*
*4th Jodie – 15.2%*
*3rd Susanne – 16.1%*
**2nd Brian – 16.8%**
**1st Kirsty – 19.9%**

Kirsty is shocked by the result – elated, but still shocked. 'I thought it was just the judges,' she says – three tipped her this week. 'I thought they'd had a few gins.'

Lots of the girls are crying, oh, it's just too much! Ant and Dec are on hugging duties and the contestants' mums and dads are giving a lot of support. Susanne – pipped by only 0.7% by Brian, is still thrilled to be in the top three – what a nice bird. Still, the secret is out this week – somehow – that this year there'll be a 'wildcard' show; eight contestants will come back to sing and the two winners will join the final ten to make the final twelve.

If you're asked, will you come back Susanne?
'Yes! I might not be so nervous this time!' she trills. And off they all go to the bar…

* Reference to Bruce Forsyth.
Ask your parents/someone older at a bus stop
if you don't know who this legend is.

**Jodie** – 22, Manchester
**'One Day I'll Fly Away'** (Randie Crawford)
Spent all of Monday in bed in the hotel, with her ailments.

**Kirsty** – 19, Northampton
**'Natural Woman'** (Carole King)
Now has to put her medical studies aside to be in the final ten.

**Adam** – 22, Buckinghamshire
**'Knocks Me Off My Feet'** (Stevie Wonder)
He only has one kidney, but it's 'one and a third' the size of a normal one.

**Samantha** – 21, Tamworth
**'The Power of Love'** (Jennifer Rush)
Carries round a 'lucky' cow's tooth. Ourgh. She also puts a tube of lip gloss in her boots, for easy access… (?)

**Bianca** – 21, London
**'Think Twice'** (Celine Dion)
Once worked in a posh club and met Cilla Black, who was 'lovely'.

**Susanne** – 21, Reading
**'Take Another Piece Of My Heart'** (Erma Franklin)
Was bullied at school: 'I wore glasses, had my hair in a plait and I was a bit of a bookworm, I was a classic target…' Aw.

**Brian** – 24, London
**'Amazed'** (Lonestar)
Bryan McFadden from Westlife is recording Des and Mel next door and pops in to see his old pal Brian. They know each other from Dublin.

**Maxwell** –18, Staines
**'Your Song'** (Elton John)
Our Prince William lookalike wears two watches, one on each wrist, and was in a boy band at sixteen, which Simon was interested in.

**Kelly-Marie** – 22, London
**'Endless Love'** (Lionel Richie)
Has spent £600 on 10,000 leaflets which she and her family have delivered locally, saying 'Vote Kelly-Marie!'

**Wesu** – 22, East Sussex
**'Overjoyed'** (Stevie Wonder)
His wife gave birth to their baby girl Meilani eight days after the Criterion auditions. 'I would have quit Pop Idol if she had been about to give birth,' he says.

# Heat 3

*'Look for personal style. Go to markets, mix old and new; what's important is good accessories and good shoes.' Mads the stylist's advice for the girls.*

It's a tough week. 'When I looked at the final 50 printed in a magazine,' says Suzanne, 'I circled all the ones I didn't want to be in a group with, because they were so good. And they're here!' But the mood is friendly. The ten bond with a meal on Sunday night, and a trip to the bingo – although Roxanne and Sam have to stay behind because they are too young to get in. Rachel, you see, is the chatterbox bingo caller from Merseyside and her infectious laughter and big personality (ie she never shuts up, bless) make this group forget it's one big competition.

While the others play, Roxanne and Sam are able to catch up with Kirsty at the hotel on Sunday night. 'She had loads of tips,' says Roxanne. 'Like be yourself, try not to let the nerves get hold of you. She was so pleased; she didn't expect it at all. When they called the results, she said her name over and over in her head – then she won!'

It's not just about how you sound; the judges – and the public – are very critical of your look. Mads the stylist (he's Danish, wears a jaunty cap) is fretting over Rachel's dress. She's had it made specially for her, but he thinks it's too much like 'something my niece would wear for ballet practice' so he's teaming it with a black dress to wear *over* it. Rachel is delighted, 'You're a genius!' she shrieks as she spots him with the needle and thread.

Mads' favourite contestant so far is Suzanne, 'because she knows what looks good on her.' He despairs of many of the boys' clothes: 'One guy had a shirt four sizes too big, they *all* have clothes hanging off them.' He is also not enamoured with the amount of black mini dresses the girls want to wear.

While Mads tries to sort everyone out, the vocal training continues by the piano. New mum Hayley starts blubbing when Douglas tells her to *feel* her song. 'Look down the lens and think of your baby,' he says… and she's a goner. Suzanne has to change her song, as she wanted to sing 'Think Twice', but Bianca sang it last week. It's panic stations for a while, until she finds Whitney's 'Run to You'. Almost everyone, again, is singing a ballad. This is because they're easier to sing to just a piano accompaniment. Says vocal coach Ce Ce, 'It's also easier to control the nerves on a slower song.'

Each contestant gives the *Pop Idol* team ten song suggestions up-front, with a top three of their favourites. They are given advice, but ultimately what they sing is their own choice. And it's the most difficult choice to make because even if you were to wear the perfect clothes and sing beautifully, if the song doesn't suit your voice then you're out.

Pete Waterman is the first judge on set on the big day. He wanders around saying hello to everyone. He talks about this week's contestants, saying how he predicted all the winners thus far, and how he knows what Kieran has chosen to sing, and that it's definitely the wrong song. Ant McPartlin is in the corner, talking to Kate Thornton. 'I went to a christening last weekend,' he says. 'And a woman came up to me and said, "OK, so who wins *Pop Idol*?" I told her that we're nowhere near the final vote. "Yeah yeah," she said and didn't believe me! She thought it was a fix!'

Time for the performances. And oh, we may have to repeat ourselves, but this week is *such* a tough week – there are 'three or four' at least, according to the judges, that should go through.

## The judges' verdict

Hayley has 'transformed'. Sam is 'one of the most naturally talented people in the competition' and Roxanne is 'sensational'. Yet the judges unleash their cruelty still: bubbly Rachel is 'terrible', Kieran (one of the initial favourites) is a 'pub singer' and when Kate is told she's 'not good enough' she gets teary. Yet when Marc is told he's given 'one of the strongest vocals' so far he starts sobbing!

And so the difficult wait until the results come through. And they are, in reverse order, viewers:

5th Suzanne – 7.7%
4th Kieran – 10.7%
3rd Sam – 19.4%
**2nd Roxanne – 23.5%**
**1st Marc D – 28.2%**

Marc is speechless, but for the faint cry of 'Mum!' Roxanne can only recite her catchphrase: 'Oh – my – God!' Both are stunned. 'Words can't express how I feel right now,' Marc says. Kieran is making light of his defeat, 'I'm happy! Fourth is fantastic!' but little Sam does admit to being 'gutted' – he was so close… It's Suzanne who admits she and Kieran each chose the wrong song. 'How do you know what song to pick? I spent weeks trying to decide. It's the hardest decision in the world.'

**Kate** – 21, Cumbria
**'Show Me Heaven'** (Maria McKee)
Enjoys skydiving in her spare time, 'I can jump out of a plane at 1200 ft, but I'm nervous walking into a room and facing the judges…'

**Hayley** – 22, York
**'That's What Friends Are For'** (Dionne Warwick, Gladys Knight and Stevie Wonder – yes, all together)
Only had her first child four months ago – just before her first audition. He's called Brook and he's very cute.

**Suzanne** – 19, Watford
**'Run To You'** (Whitney Houston)
Like Will Young, was the last person to audition in Manchester. 'They say lightning never strikes twice, but who knows?' she pondered.

**Roxanne** – 16, Hull
**'Beautiful'** (Christina Aguilera)
Loves UB40 and was sent a text on Saturday night by Robin from the band, saying 'You're a class singer'. Wow wee.

**Marc D** – 22, Ilford
**'Easy'** (The Commodores)
Is in an S Club and Steps tribute band. And he's done Robbie too. And Boyzone and Blue covers. 'But I don't want to be a tribute to anything!' he says. He wants to be a Pop Idol, of course.

**Rachel** – 22, Merseyside
**'Sitting On The Dock Of The Bay'** (Otis Redding)
Used to work on, ahem, 'adult' phone lines. When she was due to clock off, she'd tell callers she was wearing dowdy clothes to make the call quicker, so she could go home.

**Amy** – 19, Romford
**'Get Here'** (Oleta Adams)
Won £100,000 on TV show Boys and Girls. Amongst other things, she bought a pot of face cream that cost £1,000!

**Kieran** – 18, Musselburgh
**'Goodnight Girl'** (Wet Wet Wet)
Treated himself to a facial before Teddington, getting his eyebrows waxed. 'And the woman who did it had never heard of Pop Idol!' he exclaims.

**Michael** – 23, London
'**Always And Forever**' (Luther Vandross)
Tried to bleach his teeth white… and then fell asleep! 'It was meant to be for ten minutes, and it was five hours!' Consequently, his throat feels a bit rough (but his teeth are still in).

**Sam** – 17, Barnsley
**'Walking In Memphis'** (Marc Cohn)
Got an email from Andy Scott Lee, wishing him the best of luck – they'd made friends at the Criterion auditions.

# Heat 4

*'A big smile makes the judges think, "Ooh, they're having a good time." Don't show your nerves, even if you are nervous...'* Advice from Ant McPartlin

There aren't a lot of big smiles this week. Perhaps it's because the weather's suddenly turning a bit cold. Or perhaps it's the thought of the judges. Whatever it is, it's hard to make the ten look like they are having a good time... Even Tarek – yes, Tarek – is being very serious and trying not to act the goat. Kim is a little more jolly, until she spots an email from her three kids and starts blubbing...

*Pop Idol* top-tenner Hayley Evetts pops in to say hello on Monday – to wish everyone good luck. As did her ex-beau Gareth Gates... well, he was going to, but he had hardly got through the door when the nerves got him. 'It reminds me of when I was here,' he says. 'And it's too much!'

Now it's Tuesday, and Douglas, the piano accompanist with very well-conditioned hair, is sober about this week's lot. 'The singing teachers were a bit suicidal last night,' he says. 'But today is a lot better. Some of the contestants didn't seem to be interested in singing. They were rushing back to watch themselves on ITV2.' Everyone by now has made their song choice; but when they came in on Monday morning, according to Douglas, 'A lot of them come and say, "My mum has told me to sing this song for her…"'

It's not just Douglas and the vocal coaches that are feeling a bit down. Kate Thornton, splendid anchor of the ITV2 coverage, is muted about this week too. 'It's going to be an interesting one,' she says. 'The last three weeks, they'd all done their homework, they'd all seen the programme – but this lot haven't even watched last week's show.' She is trying to gee up the contestants, as they play a game with a giant dice. 'Don't be afraid to smile and look like you want to be here,' she says to our poker-faced wannabes.

They're all waiting for Darius to phone in and wish them luck and talk to Kate, but he's nowhere to be found. After fifteen minutes of waiting, it transpires that he is tucked up in bed with flu, unable to speak. Well, it makes a change, and get better soon, Darius. So last week's near-winner Sam comes on the phone and tells everyone to make the most of the week. 'I wish I was down there now!' he parples.

Kate gets stopped all the time to talk about *Pop Idol*. 'I get home, my friends ring me about the show, then there's a knock on the door and people from the end of my street are asking how it's going. I went out to an award ceremony and Emma Bunton was telling me she was tired – not because of her busy schedule, but because she'd been up all night watching the ITV2 *Pop Idol* repeats.'

Every Wednesday – without Ce Ce and John – Douglas is the man to accompany the contestants' songs when they record Saturday's show. He feels the strain. 'There's only one take, so I have to get it right too. I'm under pressure not to let them down; I'm the only friendly face in the studio that day.' This Wednesday, as every other week, everyone is tense. Kim has been practising like mad, but some are a little tired... Laura and Leon were spotted last night in the bar (Laura enjoyed a few 'lemonades'), and some say they were holding hands. Ooh! 'No comment,' is all Leon will say. Come on fellas, you've got a show to do! A competition to win!

The judges arrive and are talking about Marc, who was in the papers all this week for having had a criminal record. 'He's done his time, he's sorry,' says Pete, fairly. But then he says it's Tarek who should be doing hard labour, because he can be such a ham! 'He's a very good looking young man,' counters Nicki. And he's always controversial, even though he's been so quiet and studied these past couple of days. (He is *very* nervous.)

Simon arrives, finally, and the show begins. And oh – who is going to pull it off tonight? Who will go from ropey to radiant? From fazed to fabulous?

## The judges' verdict

'You look like a cod on a fishmonger's slab,' Simon Cowell is not mincing his words when he speaks to Laura: 'Your eyes are totally and utterly dead.' Gadzooks! – does he need to be so harsh? Elizabeth is called 'cabaret', Kim is likened to Jane McDonald, Jamie is 'bland', David 'lacked sparkle' and Tarek is told his vocal was the 'worst ever'. Yet Leon is told he has a beautiful voice by Nicki, hurrah! Off camera, Simon tells them that none of them should have been in the final fifty. They're not very happy about that one, but they mooch about, rather than try and set fire to Simon's head. The spirit, indeed, is not really here this week.

And thus the results come in. And they are, fine readers:

*5th Tarek – 8.4%*
*4th Jamie – 8.7%*
*3rd Becca – 15.5%*
**2nd Kim – 24.2%**
**1st Leon – 28.6%**

This is fortunate for Foxy, who said that if Tarek got into the final ten he would walk down Oxford Street in Kate Thornton's underwear. Leon is teary, and so's Kim. So is Ce Ce, but for other reasons. 'I am disappointed,' she says. 'It was not good enough.' Let's hope next week's Pop Idollers deliver the goods, eh?

**David** – 19, South Wales
**'What Makes A Man'** (Westlife)
Stylist Mads was not impressed by David's collection of rugby shirts, and made him go out and buy something new.

**Kim** – 23, Grimsby
**'Son of a Preacher Man'** (Dusty Springfield)
Has line-danced with dance legend Lionel Blair for Warner holidays, when she worked/sang there.

**Becca** – 16, Hailsham, Sussex
**'Without You'** (Charlie Wilson, Harry Nilsson, Mariah Carey)
Was sent an email by Pop Idol top-tenner Kirsty wishing her luck. They had met at the Criterion auditions.

**Tarek** – 25, London
**'Let Me Entertain You'** (Robbie Williams)
Was born in the basement of a Beirut hospital whilst it was being bombed. He survived to entertain us all.

**Leon** – 20, London
**'You Are Not Alone'** (Boyzone)
Leon was sent an email which said 'I love you' x about 300, and the name and phone number of a young lady. To say she was slightly enthralled is an understatement.

**Sarah** – 17, Maidenhead
**'Stuck In The Middle With You'** (Stealers Wheel, Louise)
Was selected to go to a gymnastics seminar held by Olga Korbut, a very famous gymnast, when she was ten. She's very bendy.

**Elizabeth** – 20, Liverpool
**'Still The One'** (Shania Twain)
Once worked in a shoe shop – the worst thing was all the smelly feet.

**Laura** – 19, Liverpool
**'Killing Me Softly'** (Roberta Flack, The Fugees, Luther Vandross)
Is learning to read the Tarot. Spooks!

**Jamie** – 22, Middlesbrough
**'Right Here Waiting'** (Richard Marx)
Was in the running for the UK Eurovision entry two years ago, but was beaten by Jessica Garlick.

**Danielle** – 18, Nottinghamshire
**'When I Fall In Love'** (Nat King Cole, Natalie Cole, Celine Dion)
Sang in front of 10,000 people when she performed at Chesterfield Open Air Bonanza.

*'I think they're all fabulous this week, there's a better variety of songs, and some quirky songs you wouldn't expect' Douglas, piano accompanist*

Ah, the last week of the final 50. Fair brings a tear to the old eye. Even Craig from Edinburgh was crying last night, but that was because of his choice of song. He tried 'You've Got A Friend', but it didn't quite work, and now he's back to his old standard, 'I Believe I Can Fly'.

This week, the vocal coaches think, is a close one. Everyone has been working very hard, although Ce Ce has to tell Glen not to do a Chris Hide and over-sing. The ten started out the week with a quick warm up of 'The Lion Sleeps Tonight' – guaranteed to get everyone laughing. The group is bonding well and they are all a bit 'week three' – quietly determined to do their damnedest on performance night.

Each ten has been completely different, thus far – and some weeks, as we know, far stronger than others. How do the production team choose the weeks? 'It's a random mix,' says associate producer Jo Brock. 'We have to have a good mix of boys and girls, they have to come from different areas of the country and we have to have varied styles of singers in one week.' Only one person had a holiday booked for the *Pop Idol* team to schedule around this year, and as most of the contestants are students, it's easier for them to get time off. 'And we've never had any problems from anyone's boss… not so far,' says Jo.

The contestants, as you will have noticed, are all very well behaved. They have a briefing on Sunday evening at their hotel in Teddington, during which they're told what happens over the next few days. They're also reminded not to swear, not to wear T-shirts with big brand logos on the front (no advertising) and told to switch off their mobile phones – which Katy forgets to do and it goes off live on ITV2. Kate Thornton takes the call. It's Katy's sister, wondering how it's going... she'll have to wait.

In the studio, the ten take turns to go through their songs and refine them. Ce Ce is *still* making everyone sing into water bottles; and they are very special water bottles, because the label has been ripped off each and every one – the no-advertising rule. Elizabeth is not sure whether she's nervous or not. 'It's been more stressful at home, watching the show,' she says. 'Now I'm here, everyone's really mellow. But I am dreading Saturday, I'm not going to deny it.'

Andy is a familiar face. Enjoying a short career in the band 3SL with his brothers, he was persuaded to go on *Pop Idol* series two by his sister, Lisa Scott-Lee. His girlfriend, Michelle Heaton

from Liberty X, was not so sure in case he got bad press. 'I'm pleased now,' he says, wearing a tea cosy hat. 'I was very scared.' Although Pete didn't want to judge him at his first audition, because he knew sister Lisa, Andy claims he doesn't know Pete. Even Simon claims he doesn't know Pete when they start arguing.

It's Wednesday, and the contestants have to get their glad rags on and prepare for the cameras. Tamsin says, 'It looks like a different room!' when she enters the studio, which has been rearranged. Jonathan, the director of Wednesday's (broadcast Saturday) show is on hand to let the contestants know what they're in for when they stand on that scary platform. 'Don't chase the red light,' he says – (in case you didn't already know, the camera that's filming has a red light on the top, but there are loads of cameras and the red light flits between each one. If you start to follow it, you'll lose it and end up looking around like a dizzy pigeon.) 'Your eyes are what sells a performance,' he continues, reminding some not to close their peepers when they perform. Each singer has fifteen – count 'em – minutes to rehearse. Gulp! It's not much.

Nicki and Pete are first through the door, sitting at their desk to give an opinion of the show before it starts. Foxy comes in later, then, of course, it's Simon, who's been filming *American Idol* in Hawaii, of all places. They are looking forward to this week and they sit with *Pop Idol* mugs filled with delicious hot drinks in front of them. But remember, production team and contestants, you have been warned that nicking these mugs is a 'sackable offence', so paws off.

# The judges' verdict

The standard is high; it's so very high. That's perhaps why the judges can be so 'honest'. Little Becky is told the competition is too big for her; Katy's style is called 'cruise ship'; Tamsin is 'just above average'; and Tina 'distinctly average'. But lo, she's heard that one before (Mr Will Young was told that line) and she answers back – hoorah. But Danielle is told she's 'given herself a chance'; Mark is 'blinding'; Andy is a 'nice person' (hang on, is this Personality Idol?); and Glen will 'breeze through into the top ten'. Lawks! It's time to wait for the public to get a-votin'.

The results come through. Here they are, percentage lovers:
*5th Tina – 6.9%*
*4th Glen – 15.1%*
*3rd Danielle – 17.5%*
**2nd Mark R – 20.3%**
**1st Andy – 21.1%**

The top five, apparently, were swapping places throughout the voting. It's been very, very close. Andy is so delighted he 'can't speak'. Mark is worried he's perspiring. Everyone is sad that the whole thing is over.

But hang on… it's not.

Because tonight is the night the wildcards are announced. Eight lucky people get the chance to go through the most nerve-wracking experience ever (except moving house and having a birthday party) again! Are they mad? Yes they are, they are mad with talent and determination. And you, reader, must turn over the page to remind yourself who exactly those eight are…

**Elizabeth** – 21, North London
**'When I Need You'** *(Luther Vandross, Rod Stewart, Celine Dion among others)*
*Used to wear a hearing aid in her left ear as a child.*

**Craig** – 22, Edinburgh
**'I Believe I Can Fly'** *(R Kelly)*
*Sings with a team of… strippers. Loads of ladies email in saying they've spotted him performing (with all his clothes on, mind).*

**Glen** – 18, Hampshire
**'A Million Love Songs'** *(Take That)*
*Is studying 'vocals' in Harrow. It's been a lot of theory, apparently, and 'not much singing' so far.*

**Andy** – 23, London
**'Careless Whisper'** *(George Michael)*
*Worked at a holiday camp years ago and he had to dress up as the Pink Panther, and pose with holidaymakers.*

**Danielle** – 19, Barrow-In-Furness
**'Fields Of Gold'** *(Sting)*
*Has zillions of sports awards at home, she's played hockey for the North of England Under 21 team.*

**Tina** – 23, Kent
**'Don't Want To Miss A Thing'** *(Aerosmith)*
*Was once in a show, forgot the words to a song so pretended she knew the song in Spanish and bluffed it.*

**Katy** – 23, Surrey
**'Desperado'** *(Eagles)*
*Goes leafleting with Helen O'Brien from the top 50, selling garden products. She knows how you can get a nice lawn.*

**Mark R** – 22, Walsall
**'She's Like The Wind'** *(Patrick Swayze)*
*Once met Noddy Holder from Slade and won Battle Of The Bands in the Midlands.*

**Becky** – 17, South Wales
**'You Might Need Somebody'** *(Randy Crawford)*
*Works in an ice cream parlour (The second best job in the world?). And she has a footballer boyfriend (Under 19s).*

**Tamsin** – 23, East London
**'Hero'** *(Bonnie Tyler)*
*Was in Boy George's stage show Taboo; she's still not sure whether she prefers theatre or pop.*

# Fifty become...Twelve
# Wildcard Week

'Tonight I feel I got the best moment of Pop Idol so far'
Pete Waterman

It's perhaps the most exciting week yet in *Pop Idol*. Eight contestants have got a second chance and two will make it through to the final twelve who start rehearsing and performing at the Fountain Studios, Wembley, next week. We know them by now, but how will they cope with the extra pressure?

The eight who are selected by the judges are:

| | |
|---|---|
| *Susanne* | *Danielle* |
| *Rebecca* | *Jodie* |
| *Kieran* | *Glen* |
| *Sam* | *Jason* |

It's a veritable supergroup. But why eight people? Why not ten? Or six? Says Claire Horton, bigwig producer, 'Unfortunately there's not a very exciting answer, eight people in the show mean that we can spend more time with them and get to know their characters better.'

Rebecca sits in the canteen at lunchtime on Thursday and remembers hearing the names read out on Saturday night, live on air: 'We had a rehearsal, and the production team had to read out eight names and pretend they'd gone through,' she says. 'Kelly-Marie saw her name on some sheet and thought she'd actually gone through.'

Everyone is musing upon the surreal nature of this week: here they are again, fighting for a place, but, this time, the stakes have been raised. Pop is a strange business, fans, so they better get used to it.

'Can you put, "From the writer of the *Pop Idol* book: Glen is my personal favourite. He's very charming."' Young Mr Harvey is attempting to get some special treatment from the Official (Rather Wonderful) *Pop Idol* Book. And of course he can, if he takes the author out for a swanky lunch. Alas this fails to happen, so the book will have to say that *all eight* this week are particularly fine individuals and they all deserve to go through. Ce Ce and John are very pleased that they're working with some old favourites. 'We've got more time to work with everyone, one-to-one,' says John. 'They're hungry for it...'

'Is this Des and Mel?' Lesley Joseph – from TV's *Birds of a Feather* – has popped into the green room by mistake. She scurries out again before Glen can make her say he's her favourite Pop Idoller. He's busy playing piano with Sam, and they've started on a Savage Garden medley, while Jodie and Kieran sing along. Jodie is so pleased to be better this week, 'All I was before was "the ill one"...' she sighs.

Susanne is sitting in the green room looking at a magazine. 'It's not that much different this week, but I'm happier to be here,' she says. 'Every day is so full; it's a bit like a youth centre – but without everybody fancying each other. I'm surprised there hasn't been more love...' And speaking of lurve, this week the glossy-haired sex symbol Douglas has been replaced. Oh no! Instead of his piano the contestants are accompanied by a backing track. On Sunday morning they all went to the recording studio and got the track down to 70 seconds. Then very talented studio engineers created eight unique backing tracks from scratch (which took till Tuesday), using the finest musicians and the latest equipment. Each contestant has their track on CD and they listen to them when they're not talking to Kate Thornton about their most intimate secrets on ITV2.

For the first time, the Pop Idollers are singing live on the Saturday. They are crazy with nerves, but really revved up, like eight very sporty mopeds – who are great at singing.

The judges arrive and are excited too. This should be the best show in series 2 yet. But anxiety is as anxiety does, and nerves seem to have got to these young hopefuls.

## The judges' verdict

Kieran is called 'cheesy'. Jodie is only 'adequate'. Pete is 'disappointed' in Rebecca. Glen has 'been better' and Danielle gets the old 'cabaret' line. Yet Jason is 'great', Susanne gives Pete 'goosebumps' and Sam 'ticks every box'. Corks! At least no one got to be a 'cod on a fishmonger's slab', but Simon says he's been disappointed with tonight. Ce Ce agrees that they were all better in rehearsals. Oh dear.

Results this week: one is voted in by the public, one by. the judges. Pete: 'It's been a very difficult decision, but it was unanimous [cue drum roll]… **Sam**!' Sam looks like a deeply happy young man indeed.

And the phone voting? Aargh, the agony! Who will the public want as their wildcard wonder?

| 3rd: 10.4% | Jason |
| 2nd: 16.2% | Danielle |
| 1st: 27.2% | Susanne |

'That's amazing!' Susanne utters her catchphrase once more – *aw*. Well done, lassie. 'Thank you! Thank you! And some more! Thank you!' She is overcome with emotion.

'I thought tonight was about one person – Susanne,' says Simon. 'I thought she was head and shoulders above the rest.'

'That was the problem,' says a cheery Pete.

And as the Pop Idollers drift off into the night, to celebrate, commiserate, or drink a lot, Simon can only utter a few words of solace. It's going to get even tougher.

'Next week is when the competition starts. That will be pressure, this has just been target practice.' The only target practice the Official Book can see has been the judges aiming their harsh words at the contestants. Let's hope there's no live ammunition next week…

## John and Ce Ce's most-used phrases to get the contestants into gear:

'Commit with your gestures'
'Get on top of the song'
'You are an artist, it's the frame of mind'
'You're a semitone from safety'

# Meet the Final Twelve

## ROXANNE COOPER

**Full name:** Roxanne Cooper.

**Qualifications:** Ooh, I'll have to count. I've got nine GCSEs. I've also got silver medals in disco and freestyle dancing.

**Hobbies:** Singing, dancing – disco and street dance. Hanging around with my mates.

**Can you unblock a drain?** No, I've never tried.

**First time you were recognised...** I was on the bus back in Hull, the day after my first audition, and a woman grabbed my arm and said, 'Are you Roxanne? I saw you on *Pop Idol* last night!' Since then it's been mad, I got mobbed when I went shopping. It starts with one, then someone walks past and hears my name so they come up, then other people come and see what's going on and it gets out of hand.

**Who do you most admire?** Shania Twain. She's been through hard times, and she's an original artist.

**Favourite record:** 'Red Red Wine', UB40. I emailed Robin from the group after he emailed me at Teddington, saying I'm coming to see you play in Manchester. He emailed back and said he'd see me there.

**Favourite gadget:** A penknife. I've not got one, but I think it would be useful.

**Do you have a lucky charm?** Nothing lucky. Oh actually, I found this pound coin on the floor and it's from 1986, the year I was born. I put that in my purse, I've not spent it yet.

**Can you cook?** I'm a terrible cook. I make a good bacon and egg sandwich; people like it after a night out drinking. I don't drink, I'm too young.

**Why should you be the Pop Idol?** Because I'm young, I think I have got something, there's something there that would make people like me, and I think I'd be a good role model. People my age and younger can relate to me.

**Will you be able to cope with all that cash?** We've just found out this week how much we could earn if we win. That was just – 'Oh my God, I've never heard of that much money! I can buy myself loads of clothes!' It was a big, big big amount of money.

**Can you wiggle your ears?** No, but I can roll my tongue.

**If you could be invisible for a day, what would you do?** I'd see if people were talking about me, some people back in Hull... just to check it out.

**Do you read your press?** I do, but not everything. It's a bit scary, but it's good to know people like you that much and you're in national newspapers.

**What can't you live without?** My mobile phone; it's the only way to keep in touch with people when you're on the move. I think I'd panic if I lost it, then I'd put out a search party to try and find it.

**Are you eating properly?** I am, but I've just eaten a Galaxy bar. I love them. My dad's here to make sure I'm OK.

**What are the three most vital things in your suitcase?** Toothbrush, clean socks and my teddy bears. I've got about twenty in my suitcase.

**What was the last thing you bought but didn't wear?** Last time I was in London at the Criterion auditions, I was nagging for this Kangol hat, and it's not even been on my head yet. It cost £30.

**If you were stuck in a lift with the judges, who would you prefer?** I'd choose Simon, because I think he'd be good to talk to, he's always got something to say, he's interesting and quite brainy. I'd ask him who he thinks will win *Pop Idol*.

**Draw your idea of fame:**

# KIRSTY CRAWFORD

**Full name:** Kirsty Ann Crawford. I was going to be called Christiana, but my mum was sympathetic to me in the end.

**Qualifications:** I have ten GSCEs, one AS Level, five A Levels: general studies, biology, chemistry, maths and further maths.

**Hobbies:** Singing and dancing. I love playing field hockey, but I haven't played it for a while. I like doodling, making things, being arty. I miss school for that, you had to do things. I couldn't tell you a thing from further maths.

**Can you unblock a drain?** I'm a woman, magic touch.

**First time you were recognised…**
In my local supermarket, I used to work there in customer services. An elderly gentleman said to me recently, when I went in there, 'Why aren't there any more chocolate digestives in here?' I said, 'I've told you this countless times, I don't work here any more!' He said, 'I thought you were making it up.' People think customer services lie all the time.

**Who do you most admire?** Robbie Williams, I love him as an entertainer, he's funny, he's smart, creative and very good at what he does. Vocally I admire gospel Whitney, Avril Lavigne. I admired Geri Halliwell when she left The Spice Girls, because she was a UN ambassador.

**Favourite record:** I love a track from the movie *The Preacher's Wife* called 'I Believe In You And Me', sung by Whitney Houston. I love soundtracks.

**Favourite gadget:** My mobile phone. I'd love a video camera, so much.

**Do you have a lucky charm?** My boyfriend gave me an eternity ring that I always keep. I have to have that facing forward when I sing. I also have a shoelace bracelet, which is really unattractive and goes with nothing but is very lucky. I always make sure I have something from my friends when I sing.

**Can you cook?** Yes. The best thing I've cooked is Mediterranean risotto. But my speciality is pasta in chicken stock or jam on toast. The jam has to be Hartleys or above. Bon Maman is very good, and the jam you get in Spain.

**Why should you be the Pop Idol?**
I wouldn't like to set myself above the rest, but the only reason it would be good to have me at the top would be because I can't do arrogant. I would never be a diva. I like being cheeky – I'd love to run on in the middle of *Parkinson*, give him a kiss and run off again. I'd be like Ginger Spice. At the end of the day it makes people smile. I think the entertainment's been lost out of singing.

**Will you be able to cope with all that cash?** No. I'm giving it to my dad, 'Will you please look after this?' We have to sort out tax, that scares the Bejesus out of me. Amongst other things, I'd like to get a bouncy castle though.

**Can you wiggle your ears?** Only if I use my hands. I can flare my nostrils. If my boyfriend is in a *pretend* mood, I do it and he goes, 'Oh you berk.'

**If you could be invisible for a day, what would you do?** Ooh, I'd go into Buckingham Palace and see how the day actually goes. I'd love to be an SAS person too.

**Do you read your press?** Yes. I worry a lot about how people see me, so I do read it. I learnt from the last press incident to keep your boobs covered. I was wearing that low-cut dress….

**What can't you live without?** My friends and family, I *really* couldn't live without them. And a pen and paper, because I love to doodle.

**Are you eating properly?** Yes! Well – we've been having a lot of bread. I'm not a big fan of chocolate, I like pick 'n' mix sweets, hence the tooth fillings. I'd like to be famous because I'd like to be able to afford dental treatment.

**What are the three most vital things in your suitcase?** I normally forget vital things. My underwear – I don't like wearing it twice. Blusher, I'm not a girly girl, but I realise if you're having a pale day you can dust it over your face. And my new polka dot skirt, and my mobile phone.

**What was the last thing you bought but didn't wear?** A top from Top Shop that had a hole in it, I have to take it back. And the other thing I did buy is a lovely red skirt, salsa style, it's lovely but it's not trendy, for a night out.

**If you were stuck in a lift with the judges, who would you prefer?** I think I might hurt Pete – no, I *do* like him… he's just been the only one that said negative stuff. Nicki – she's a very nice person. But Foxy would make me laugh. Foxy, then.

**Draw your idea of fame:**

# MARC DILLON

**Full name:** Marc Owen Dillon.

**Qualifications:** Normal Scottish standard grades. I was more of a maths person than arts.

**Hobbies:** Football, I'm mad for football; I play midfield. And I'm a Celtic fan.

**Can you unblock a drain?** Yes. All depends on what kind of drain you're talking about. You get the rods out, open the manhole, and get in there.

**First time you were recognised…**
Monday after my heat, because I did *This Morning*. I got home, went up to my local shop, Chadz, where I get my clothes. I got out the car, wham! I was hounded. I had to run into a shop to try and get away from it. One guy said, 'Can you phone my wife?' I said, 'No, I don't know her…' But he phoned her anyway.

**Who do you most admire?** My mum. She's been through a lot, she's done a lot with her life. Peace and respect.

**Favourite record:** 'Flying Without Wings' by Westlife.

**Favourite gadget:** Laptop computers, anything with a DVD player.

**Do you have a lucky charm?** I did have lucky boxer shorts that I had since I was twelve, they were torn and ripped but I used to wear them. I walked into the house and Mandy's – my girlfriend – mum was mopping the floor with them.

**Can you cook?** I can do a nice spag bol, tagliatelle. My *pièce de résistance* is frying steak. To get it nicely done, I'd say give it ten minutes.

**Why should you be the Pop Idol?** Because I love it, I love to be on stage. I love to perform and be idolised. I love to sing to people who are enjoying my music.

**Will you be able to cope with all that cash?** Not a problem. I've got a fiancée who would love it. All I want is my white Ferrari Spider. My money is going to go into property. I want to know I'll always have something to fall back on.

**Can you wiggle your ears?** Yes, I can!

**If you could be invisible for a day, what would you do?** Go to the FBI and MI5 and see if there were any real secrets. Who shot Kennedy? Did Diana really die in a car accident?

**Do you read your press?** Yes. [There were stories aplenty printed about Marc's criminal past after his Teddington heat.] Then we went on holiday and not one paper was opened, came back, and there was nothing. It was great. I was scared of what people thought of me, but I was wrong to think that. My family, friends and neighbours have all been fantastic.

**What can't you live without?** Television. And films.

**Are you eating properly?** I have fruit in the mornings, and junk food during the day… but I'm a healthy eater really.

**What are the three most vital things in your suitcase?** Designer clothes. There a company I get my clothes off, they do the

smaller designer companies. Hair gel and T-shirts.

**What was the last thing you bought but didn't wear?** A black T-shirt with a baby on it. I had a yellow one, which I wore on my heat, and a black one.

**If you were stuck in a lift with the judges, who would you prefer?** Simon Cowell. To talk with him, to see what he's really like as a person. I'd like to know more about him. The *real* Simon Cowell.

**Draw your idea of fame:**

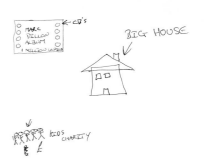

# KIM GEE

**Full name:** Kimberly Ann Gee.

**Qualifications:** I've got thirteen GCSEs, and an HND in music production. I can work a mixing desk.

**Hobbies:** I like collecting pocket dragons, little ornaments. They're green, cute dragons. My dad built a cabinet for them. I'll never be sick of them.

**Can you unblock a drain?** Yeah, I get the Mr Muscle out.

**First time you were recognised...** The Monday after the show, I went into town with my mum and my kids and everybody was walking past saying 'That's her out of *Pop Idol*!' Not very discreet really.

**Who do you most admire?** Marilyn Monroe. Because, as people probably know in this series, there's quite a debate about image versus talent and she's the perfect example – she was a size sixteen and she was one of the sexiest women in the world.

**Favourite record:** There's so many. Have to say my old favourite, 'Kiss From A Rose' by Seal.

**Favourite gadget:** My new watch. I got it from New Look, £2.99. It's a bangle type one; I can wear it with my other bangles.

**Do you have a lucky charm?** I have lucky jewellery that I've worn every audition. It's something my mum brought me from New York. A big thick rope of silver chain, and then earrings with diamante. So far I've got through every audition.

**Can you cook?** Yes, but my husband would probably disagree. My speciality is sausage pasta. Grill the sausages, chop them up, make the pasta and put a jar of tomato sauce in there, then you mix it all up. Melt cheese on it, and it's luscious.

**Why should you be the Pop Idol?** Because it's a good example of someone coming from nowhere, I've got more against me than anyone else. I've got children; there are no people who started their career who've had children. Kym Marsh fibbed about it, you see. And then there's the obvious one, I'm not the stereotypical image of a pop star. It's not Pop Icon, it's *Pop Idol* – someone who you respect and admire.

**Will you be able to cope with all that cash?** There's Oprah Winfrey's famous quote: 'When you can't spend any more money on yourself, it becomes a game as to what you can do with it.' I'd give it to charity, start my own company, try and benefit other people.

**Can you wiggle your ears?** No. I'm not even going to try. I can roll my tongue.

**If you could be invisible for a day, what would you do?** Go and set up camp in the Leeds United dressing room. Alan Smith! Woooargh! He's lush. When I found I got through to the final 50, my husband sent an email to Leeds, they were playing a home game. They announced on the telly that I was a diehard Leeds fan and going to be on the programme soon. Ten thousand Leeds fans went, 'Yeeeaaargh!'

**Do you read your press?** Yes, you get quite upset by it. Everything I've read has said I'm lucky to get through. When the odds came out, I was a complete outsider. Most of the time, I don't care, but sometimes I think it would be nice to have someone backing me.

**What can't you live without?** Shampoo. I can't stand having greasy hair.

**Are you eating properly?** Junk food. But I had pasta salad for my lunch – I'm eating, but whether I'm eating sensibly I don't know.

**What are the three most vital things in your suitcase?** Hairbrush, shampoo of course – I like Pantene Wash 'N' Go – and a picture of my kids.

**What was the last thing you bought but didn't wear?** A red shirt, to go with my white suit. It was really frilly, unflattering, but I was rushing around... once I got it home, I didn't even put it on. It was £25 and all!

**If you were stuck in a lift with the judges, who would you prefer?** Nicki. She's lovely, she's very straight talking, and she always finds something to talk about. She's opinionated but in a nice way. And she smells nice.

**Draw your idea of fame:**

# CHRIS HIDE

**Full name:** Christopher John Hide.

**Qualifications:** I've my GCSEs, AS Levels and A Levels in theatre studies, performing arts and music.

**Hobbies:** Mainly music related; that's everything I do. I play tenor sax, alto sax, and I can play the piano but I haven't *properly* learnt. I played clarinet when I was eight.

**Can you unblock a drain?** No. I wouldn't have a clue. But I'm willing to learn new things.

**First time you were recognised…** One time I was sitting on the train and I had my sunglasses on. Two people had their newspapers right up by their faces, and they're whispering, and they looked over the top of their papers, and it was blatantly obvious they were talking about me. You don't know what to do, you sit there… it wasn't subtle.

**Who do you most admire?** I do admire my dad. He's done really well for himself.

**Favourite record:** I love 'Beauty and The Beast'.

**Favourite gadget:** I'm not a very gadgety person. I've got two phones, my new one and my old one. I love my phones.

**Do you have a lucky charm?** No, not really.

**Can you cook?** Yeah. I did go through a stage of wanting to cook at home all the time. Roast dinners, proper stuff. My family liked it, yeah.

**Why should you be the Pop Idol?** We're all totally different from what's out there already. I don't sound like anybody. No one here does. I've calmed my riffs down; I think the nerves got me on that first Teddington week.

**Will you be able to cope with all that cash?** I don't see why not, I've never had that much. I've always wanted a baritone sax. I've brought my alto sax with me, a smaller one, it's in my hotel room. I want a grand piano too.

**Can you wiggle your ears?** No, I can't.

**If you could be invisible for a day, what would you do?** It's not a quality I'd like to have. Telepathy would be much more interesting.

**Do you read your press?** Yes, they all have their opinions. Half of them have one opinion; the others are the opposite. What can't you live without? My friends and people who care about me. And music.

**Are you eating properly?** Yeah. I think so. This morning I got up quite late and didn't have breakfast, but other than that it's been fine. I've been having a good big breakfast most days.

**What are the three most vital things in your suitcase?** My razor, my contact lenses and socks.

**What was the last thing you bought but didn't wear?** I don't buy loads of clothes, so I wear them all. We did go shopping yesterday for stuff. I never pick anything too *out there*, it's usually quite normal.

**If you were stuck in a lift with the judges, who would you prefer?** Probably Pete, because… he would be the person who'd most like to listen to me sing. I'd spend the time trying to impress him.

**Draw your idea of fame:**

# MICHELLE McMANUS

**Full name:** Michelle Helen McManus.

**Qualifications:** I've got seven standard grades, three highers in English, music and French. I went straight into hotels, and then I moved into event management for Marriot.

**Hobbies:** I love swimming, for fun more than anything. Obviously singing and I play the violin – very badly.

**Can you unblock a drain?** Yes, I have unblocked a drain. I live in a flat with other females and we've just worked out how to change a light bulb as well. I don't want to show off or anything…

**First time you were recognised…** A personal trainer walked up to me in the street and proceeded to try and have a half-hour chat with me about what I should be doing. I didn't know this guy from Adam and he didn't introduce himself as a personal trainer till halfway through – I had to say, 'Do I know you?' He actually got down, in

the middle of the street, to show me how to do squats.

**Who do you most admire?** I'm not a political person so I don't get involved in that. Madonna, because nothing gets her down, she'll keep coming back. She's not scared to reinvent herself, to change her image. She's the most successful female artist ever.

**Favourite record:** I've got loads of favourite records. At the moment, my favourite band is The Darkness. I saw them in Glasgow, they're a wicked band. My favourite song of all time is 'From This Moment' by Shania Twain.

**Favourite gadget:**
I think electric car park gates are fantastic, but I don't drive. I've got an electric pencil sharpener, which I use in the office when I'm bored.

**Do you have a lucky charm?** I don't have lucky charms. I always wear rings when I'm singing; I will never go on stage unless I've got some sort of ring. A fortune teller once told me a ring was my lucky charm. Doesn't have to be the same ring either.

**Can you cook?** No, absolutely not. I almost killed my flatmates with a pasta bake. Don't ask me how I did it. All I did was pour the sauce on pasta and they were all very ill after it.

**Why should you be the Pop Idol?**
Because I'm dedicated and at the end of the day, I'm not in this to get publicity. It's a competition for me, and I'm in it to win. It's not so I can get chucked out and someone will pick me up. This is it for me, I've never wanted to do anything else.

**Will you be able to cope with all that cash?** Just about. I may feel a bit pressured sometimes, having all that money in my bank account. I'm going to buy a nice car I can look at, 'cos I can't drive and no one will teach me. I'm pathetic at it, my driving instructor asked me not to come back.

**Can you wiggle your ears?** No. I've got a short tongue so I can't touch my nose with it either.

**If you could be invisible for a day, what would you do?** Go to David Beckham's dressing room and never leave.

**Do you read your press?** Yeah, I do read it, at the moment. A guy I knew years ago, a flatmate, went to the papers to say I broke his heart and I stole all his money. We never even went out, we were just friends. Complete load of crap, really.

**What can't you live without?** My GHD straighteners 'cos I look like a poodle without them. It's a nightmare, a bit of rain on you, that's you home for the night.

**Are you eating properly?** I'm on WeightWatchers so I've got a great diet, I've lost four and a half stone on it. But I haven't eaten for two days, I've been ill.

**What are the three most vital things in your suitcase?** Underwear, straighteners and bronzer. Trusty bronzer.

**What was the last thing you bought but didn't wear?** A hideous lace shirt, which looked really good on the hanger, I took it home and put it on and I looked like, ahem, *a lady of the evening*.

**If you were stuck in a lift with the judges, who would you prefer?** I really like Simon Cowell but I prefer Nicki Chapman. I'd chat about girly things, hair products she's using, where she likes going shopping.

**Draw your idea of fame:**

# LEON McPHERSON

**Full name:** Leon Paul McPherson.

**Qualifications:** I've got five GCSEs, I've passed GNVQ and AVCE art and design. I got into London College of Fashion and I had to turn it down for this.

**Hobbies:** Dancing, reading – Anne Rice novels about vampires. I love horror movies. I love shopping, being mad, spending time with my mum.

**Can you unblock a drain?** I cannot, but there's this stuff that is the best. My drain got blocked at home and I went to the top of the road, and got this liquid, it dissolves everything – it burns your skin if you touch it.

**First time you were recognised...** I was at the bus stop going to work, my cleaning job, cleaning toilets. Someone said, 'Are you that boy off *Pop Idol*?' I said 'Yeah.' If I had said no, they might have thought I was stuck up. It's not that, I'm just shy.

**Who do you most admire?** I most admire my mum, she rises above every situation. She's a single parent, she's always been there 100%.

She tells me if my dad comes around, I must be nice to him, treat him well.

**Favourite record:** Aaliyah's *One In A Million* album.

**Favourite gadget:** My DVD player, it's not that special, it just plays Aaliyah. I'm a tiny bit obsessed.

**Do you have a lucky charm?** I have this jade cross, which my friend got me from the Philippines, my best mate. I wear it all the time. But I don't believe an inanimate object will actually give me luck. I will just try and do my best.

**Can you cook?** Rice and peas and chicken. I'm really good at pasta – that's really hard, isn't it! I don't eat too many carbohydrates. I used to be sixteen stone, about two years ago. I've slimmed right down.

**Why should you be the Pop Idol?** In the beginning I didn't plan on this, I just wanted to get through the first audition. I'm not in it to be the Pop Idol, I just want someone to see me and help me. I want Sam or Michelle to be the Pop Idol.

**Will you be able to cope with all that cash?** I'd give it to Mummy, she can have it. First off I'm going to give my mum a holiday to Jamaica. Hopefully, see if we can buy our own property. Move in with Mum, my stepdad. Me and my mum are very close.

**Can you wiggle your ears?** No, I can't. I can cartwheel, though.

**If you could be invisible for a day, what would you do?** I would do so much, in America there's cheerleaders and I would run through their dressing room.

**Do you read your press?** Some of it, yeah. I think it's stupid, the things they say, it's not true. They said I was going out with a girl called Laura – who's just a girl I know.

She had to ring her boyfriend and say, 'Have you seen what's in the paper today?' All three of us were laughing, thinking, 'How pathetic are they?'

**What can't you live without?** My mum, and music. And food.

**Are you eating properly?** I do, I'm greedy, I eat loads, and the nervous energy burns it off. But I am healthy as well.

**What are the three most vital things in your suitcase?** My hair gel, my Clearasil and my mirror.

**What was the last thing you bought but didn't wear?** A pair of black shoes, they had a half-round toe, like a Taco. I hate them, but a girl told me they looked great, I've never worn them. I haven't seen the girl since; I don't speak to her any more.

**If you were stuck in a lift with the judges, who would you prefer?** Nicki. I respect her and she's honest without being rude or discouraging.

**Draw your idea of fame:**

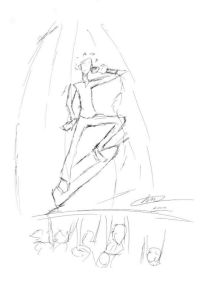

# SUSANNE MANNING

**Full name:** Susanne Manning. My middle name was nearly Mabel, but my parents neglected to put that in. My grandma was called Mabel Manning. I would like it as my first name, but not my middle name.

**Qualifications:** I've got twelve GCSEs, three A Levels and a degree in English Literature at Norwich Uni.

**Hobbies:** Shopping, possibly. I don't have proper hobbies like you do when you're a kid. I do love fashion; I spend time reading up on what's in and out. Socialising is my biggest hobby. I realised once I moved away from Uni, I have to be around people.

**Can you unblock a drain?** Don't believe so, though I have had a go once with some draining rods. My ex-ex-ex-boyfriend's house nearly flooded. And I have had some hair-in-the-plug issues at the student house I lived in; you know what it's like.

**First time you were recognised…** The first proper time was after the first ever showing of my audition. I was walking down the street, someone gave me a flyer, I took it and she said, 'Are you from *Pop Idol*?' That was very strange. It's less weird than I was expecting it to be, I thought I'd be really freaked out, but it's actually quite nice. I've had no one stop and say, 'I thought you were rubbish.'

**Who do you most admire?** [Long pause.] Nelson Mandela, people who have put things on the line and sacrificed a serious amount for not necessarily any considerable gain. People who buck the trends. Anyone who's stood up and said no.

**Favourite record:** 'Lover You Should Have Come Over' by Jeff Buckley. It's the only record that has ever made me cry listening to it. I was in floods when I heard it, the way he sings. Although no one knows him and I feel a little bit up my own bottom, he's got the most emotive voice – that's what I go for in music.

**Favourite gadget:** I'm quite a big fan of electric tin openers. I'm left-handed and the amount of time I spend trying to figure it out…

**Do you have a lucky charm?** No, I'm not superstitious, I don't believe in luck.

**Can you cook?** Yes, when I put my mind to it. But I've eaten supernoodles and jacket potatoes for three years. I'm not completely at a loss in the kitchen but I'm not amazing. I do quite a good lasagne.

**Why should you be the Pop Idol?** I think the only answer I can give – I don't have the best voice, I know that – because maybe I don't fit the Pop Idol mould.

**Will you be able to cope with all that cash?** I think I would be able to cope. I have a serious shoe habit to fund. They mocked me at Uni, now they're eating their words. Shoes, make-up. My family need some money, it would be so fantastic to say 'Here's £50,000, why don't you pay off some of your mortgage?'

**Can you wiggle your ears?** No, but I can flare my nostrils.

**If you could be invisible for a day, what would you do?** I've always had this thing about wanting to know what people actually say about me behind my back… If not I'll sneak into Dave Grohl from the Foo Fighters' dressing room.

**Do you read your press?** I don't actively look. If I know there's a new *OK!* and they have something on *Pop Idol*, perhaps… but it's already freaking me out so I don't think I'll be reading it.

**What can't you live without?** There are some very frivolous things like lip balm. But I always read my bible every day. It keeps me sane. Well, it doesn't keep me sane, I'm not a complete nut bar, but I always go back to the Good Book.

**Are you eating properly?** Too properly, the food is all so good. The breakfast here is full on. Plus they've got almond croissants, *pain au chocolat*… then there's lunch, and dinner…

**What are the three most vital things in your suitcase?** I have ten pairs of shoes with me, but they're all cheapy cheapy. My make-up case, in all. What else is vital? The right bras – strapless, halternecks, pushy-up ones…

**What was the last thing you bought but didn't wear?** I always wear everything; I have to fall in love with something to buy it. I've been skint for so long, it's a big deal to make a purchase. But saying that I have had things I haven't worn a lot.

**If you were stuck in a lift with the judges, who would you prefer?** I think Pete for sheer entertainment value. You don't know where he'd go. He has lots of rock 'n' roll stories.

**Draw your idea of fame:**

# SAM NIXON

**Full name:** Sam Nixon, not even Samuel, just Sam.

**Qualifications:** Five GCSEs, and I've finished my first year NVQ level one catering and hospitality.

**Hobbies:** I love playing guitar, trying to write songs when I can. I'm in a band called Fareview, so I play acoustic and electric. We do a lot of covers, Beatles, Queen… and we do our own music too. Obviously there's cooking, and socialising with my friends – I love chilling out with them.

**Can you unblock a drain?** Why? Ha ha! I've never done it before; I might have to be taught.

**First time you were recognised…** I can't remember. I think you get a lot of people pointing and things, it's quite strange.

Everyone's staring now. There's a girl who stands outside the hotel and, bless her, last week when I got through, she was waiting there all night and it was freezing. That's quite nice.

**Who do you most admire?** Probably Jamie Oliver, he's the one who inspired me to cook. Watching him, with him being so young, and seeing his passion for cooking. He's done a lot, to get some people who don't know anything about cooking and train them – that's amazing, that.

**Favourite record:** The John Mayer album, *Room For Squares*.

**Favourite gadget:** That's the hardest question I've had so far… I don't know. My mate bought me an alarm clock, from a gadget shop, so that.

**Do you have a lucky charm?** I've got a lucky pebble, it was given to me by my hairdresser, at the Criterion stage. It's a smooth one.

**Can you cook?** Well, yeah. I do a nice chicken dish with a creamy sauce, but the main thing is Christmas dinner, I love doing that. I've been told if I am here next week they want me to do a bit of cooking for the cameras.

**Why should you be the Pop Idol?** Because it's a job I know I'd love to do, so I'd be passionate about it, for one thing. I love performing and being on stage. I've always wanted to do it. I'm a bit of a rocker, so perhaps that's something different.

**Will you be able to cope with all that cash?** Definitely, I'd love to have a nice bank balance. Whenever I've got some money, I can't think what I want to buy, I'd probably spend it on other people.

**Can you wiggle your ears?** A bit, without scrunching up my face.

**If you could be invisible for a day, what would you do?** Ooh. Probably sneak into a big meeting where something big's happening, or go to a press office and find out things before anyone else. Max Clifford's office or something.

**Do you read your press?** I do like to read it but I don't think you should listen to it, good or bad. Talking about odds, it all depends on the night. But if I'm in the paper I do like to read it 'cos it's the first time I've ever done anything like this.

**What can't you live without?** I'd say my guitar but I've not brought it with me. I popped home, meant to bring it, but I didn't.

**Are you eating properly?** Yes. We keep having quite a few take-aways, so I might have to calm that down.

**What are the three most vital things in your suitcase?** Hair products, deodorant and clothes.

**What was the last thing you bought but didn't wear?** A pair of jeans, because they kind of fitted, but they didn't. I bought them for *Pop Idol*, but I never wore them. They were a bit too short in the leg, my socks were showing.

**If you were stuck in a lift with the judges, who would you prefer?** I can't say Nicki, because apparently I've said I fancy her.

**Draw your idea of fame:**

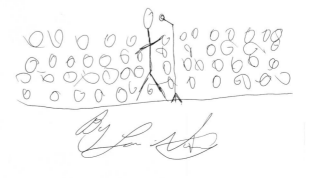

# BRIAN ORMOND

**Full name:** Brian James Simon Ormond. Simon is my confirmation name.

**Qualifications:** I was an electrician and I left before I took the final exam and qualified. I knew I had to do it. I loved it but I'd never go back.

**Hobbies?** I love soccer, going to the cinema, theatre – musicals. It's mostly soccer. I used to play in a football team back home, the Freewheelers.

**Can you unblock a drain?** I suppose I probably could. As long as the blockage wasn't too far down. I'd give it a go anyway.

**First time you were recognised…** I was in a train station one day and a girl came up to me, stared at me from literally just a few inches away, and then walked away. She went up to her friends and said, 'Yeah, it's him.' It's weird that way.

**Who do you most admire?** Andy Scott-Lee for coming on *Pop Idol*. It must have been the hardest thing ever. I've had a lot of knock-backs; I did the Irish *Popstars* but didn't get through, so I know how hard it is to get back in the queue after doing well.

**Favourite record:** I love Lionel Richie's album *Back To Front* – it's got 'Three Times A Lady', 'Stuck On You', all his hits… I love Elton John, Billy Joel. John Mayer, I love him. I listen to everything, I really do.

**Favourite gadget:** My mobile phone. I have a picture phone: it has games on. I haven't taken any of *Pop Idol* yet, but I must.

**Do you have a lucky charm?** I have two lucky medals. I always put them in my pocket when I'm singing. They're holy medals – one has Mary on it; there's Jesus on the other one.

**Can you cook?** Yeah, I'm not too bad. I love giving it a go. My godmother told me how to make this dish: you get chicken fillets, put them in the pan to brown them, then put it in a cooking tray, stock cubes, water and two tins of tomatoes, in the oven till it's cooked, bit of cheese over it. It's absolutely gorgeous.

**Why should you be the Pop Idol?** I've tried everything. On Irish *Popstars*, they picked six people and I was seventh. That was so unlucky. Also, I didn't get through to represent Ireland in Eurovision – so hopefully this is third time lucky for me.

**Will you be able to cope with all that cash?** I think I would. It wouldn't drive me mad.

**Can you wiggle your ears?** No, not unless I can wiggle them with my hands. I can do something with my teeth, but I can't show you now. If I get a bit of dental floss I could show you. It's freaky. [*Mmm*, eh readers?]

**Do you read your press?** The funniest thing that's been printed about me is that I slept with Jordan. We're great friends, that's all. I think she's great; she's two different people – Katie and Jordan. Jordan only appears when the paparazzi are outside. She loves music, she's always singing, songs like 'I'm In Chains', and 'Get Here'. She's a good singer. Nah, I don't think she should be a pop star, she's a better model.

**If you could be invisible for a day, what would you do?** I'd sit in Simon Cowell's office for the day and listen to him having a meeting about *Pop Idol*. Get the inside information.

**What can't you live without?** Music, but that's boring. I'd be lost without my mobile phone.

**Are you eating properly?** I think I am, everyone has junk food, don't they? I had fruit this morning, and then I had McDonald's for lunch.

**What are the three most vital things in your suitcase?** My mobile phone charger, my underwear – I've got loads of pants with me. And my wallet – if I didn't have my bank cards I'd be lost.

**What was the last thing you bought but didn't wear?** A jumper. I bought it a month ago, just a white jumper from Top Man. Still has the tags on it.

**If you were stuck in a lift with the judges, who would you prefer?** Nicki Chapman, because she's gorgeous.

**Draw your idea of fame:**

# MARK RHODES

**Full name:** Mark Thomas Rhodes. My parents were going to call me Mark Anthony, but that was too much like the Roman chap.

**Qualifications:** I took my GNVQ in leisure and tourism, which is equivalent to two A Levels. I did want to be an air steward, and I worked as a holiday rep as well. You try and make everyone feel welcome.

**Hobbies:** I love singing, which is quite good 'cos I'm in *Pop Idol*. I like football, playing sports when I can. I like going out with my mates and getting wrecked.

**Can you unblock a drain?** No, it's usually me that's blocking it. [?]

**First time you were recognised…** I went into my local Asda and I was at the meat counter, these two little girls were sniggering, saying 'Is it him off the telly?' I went, 'I am' and they went 'Heheeee heheheheeee!' They were about twelve. It was cool.

**Who do you most admire?** Nurses, doctors and teachers. I think anything like that. Something like this, you're not working, it's a hobby that you're good at, and you get paid for it. Doctors save lives.

**Favourite record:** *Parachutes* by Coldplay, I love that. As a song, 'With Or Without You' by U2.

**Favourite gadget:** I like the fact that my mobile phone vibrates when I've got a message. It's just gone off now, I like that, ha ha!

**Do you have a lucky charm?** I've got a lucky horseshoe, and a lucky little cube that my brother's given me. I said to him, 'Why is it lucky?' and he says, 'Well, this little man gave it to me.' I says, 'Was *he* lucky? How the hell do you know if it's lucky or not?' and he says, 'Well, I don't. Take it anyway.' He's ten years older than me, so it's even worse.

**Can you cook?** Just the usual, spag bog and stuff like that. I'm not one of those people who just stick stuff in the microwave. I like to eat properly.

**Why should you be the Pop Idol?** I think you should be the Pop Idol if you choose the right songs. And if you do them as well or better than the original. The only way you could be described as a Pop Idol is if you're taking it to another level.

**Will you be able to cope with all that cash?** I'll have good try. The first thing I'd buy would be a really nice car, I've got a Renault 5, it's like a Flintstones car, bless it. I'd get a Mercedes, I wouldn't go crazy.

**Can you wiggle your ears?** Yes, I can. [Wiggles them.]

**If you could be invisible for a day, what would you do?** I'd go into an aerobics class and sit at the back while the women are doing their stretches.

**Do you read your press?** I do, actually probably shouldn't. They're so fickle, the press, they go from one extreme to the other. I don't take any notice of it.

**What can't you live without?** My bed. I love sleeping, it's brilliant.

**Are you eating properly?** I always eat properly. I eat more than I should do, to be honest. Crisps intake is outweighing the salad intake this week, but that's always the way with me.

**What are the three most vital things in your suitcase?** My deodorant, my toothbrush and my CD player. I've brought The Darkness, *Robbie Williams Live at Knebworth*, *Dive In* by Darius – it's brill.

**What was the last thing you bought but didn't wear?** My new pants, I haven't worn them yet. I've lost my lucky pants, in the other hotel at Teddington. Somebody might have nicked them.

**If you were stuck in a lift with the judges, who would you prefer?** Pete, he's the only one who can understand my accent.

**Draw your idea of fame:**

# ANDY SCOTT-LEE

**Full name:** Robert Andrew Jason Scott-Lee.

**Qualifications:** I've got ten GCSEs and I've got three A Levels and I went to Uni for a year, studying multi-media design. Animation, special effects. I was in a band and we got a deal, so I left. I can always go back.

**Hobbies:** Magic, that's my favourite hobby, I'm more a David Blaine than Tommy Cooper. Football. That's it, really.

**First time you were recognised...** Yeah, it's not Andy from 3SL, it's Andy from *Pop Idol* now, it's weird, but I like it. I went down to watch Blaine get put in the box, we managed to get there and see it. I didn't think anyone would recognise me, it was so dark and I had a cap on, but I got spotted there.

**Who do you most admire?** My father, because he's always positive and he never gives up. I hope I've got those qualities from him.

**Favourite record:** I quite like Beyoncé's 'Crazy In Love'. I'm into Justin Timberlake, I love all his stuff.

**Favourite gadget:** I love gadgets. The favourite one is my remote control jammer. It stops my brothers or anyone turning over the channel. It was only about £5 but it works.

**Do you have a lucky charm?** Not really, I'd like to think my ring is. It's from my girlfriend, Michelle. It's got four sapphires, diamonds and it's made from white gold. [It's quite flash, readers.]

**Can you cook?** No, I'm so bad at cooking. I cooked a pancake the other day, and I didn't put enough fat in so it got stuck to the pan. I tried to flip it and it honestly did drop on the floor.

**Why should you be the Pop Idol?** Because, it's something I really want to do. I believe I have the energy, and the talent for it, hopefully. I just want to do it. We all do.

**Will you be able to cope with all that cash?** I'd like to think so, but I've never had that much cash so I don't know. We didn't have a lot when we were in 3SL. I think I'd buy my dad a car. A Porsche would be good, then I could borrow it.

**Can you wiggle your ears?** No. I can touch my nose with my tongue. I can backflip.

**If you could be invisible for a day, what would you do?** I would go and see how Simon Cowell lives, what kind of life he has, check out his properties and things.

**Do you read your press?** I think everyone does, good or bad. If it's negative I try not to pay attention to it.

**What can't you live without?** Chips. I love them.

**Are you eating properly?** I'm not, actually. The food's there, but it's such a big show, you get quite nervous so I don't feel very hungry.

**What are the three most vital things in your suitcase?** CD player, clothes and my undies.

**What was the last thing you bought but didn't wear?** A jacket, I thought it was nice but everyone else said it was awful. The pattern and the colour.

**If you were stuck in a lift with the judges, who would you prefer?** It would have to Nicki, wouldn't it?

**Draw your idea of fame:**

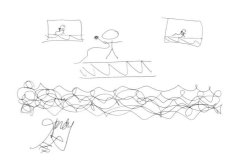

51

# How to be a Pop Idol

## By the experts...

### ANT AND DEC: The Show's Hosts

**What qualities do you need to be the Pop Idol?**

**Dec:** I think clean teeth and smart hair are a good start, heh heh! Like you're going to a job interview.

**Ant:** I think the viewers like people who are over-awed by the experience, who are quite innocent to it. You see some of them get up there and sing, and then we interview them and they say, 'It's brilliant, I've never experienced anything like this before.' It endears them to the viewers.

**Are the public more sophisticated in the way they're voting this time?**

**Dec:** I do think so. People are a lot more strategic with their votes, in a way. We've seen a lot more of people not bothering to vote, thinking that their favourite will be all right. That's cool, but at the end of the day we want to find the idol who people think is the best.

**Ant:** And this year goes on performances as well. If you have a bad week you really could go out. Last year Will, Gareth and Darius had their own fanbases, who voted for them however they did. If they had a dodgy week they'd still get the votes.

*Who's a good pop idol now?*

**Ant:** I think Robbie Williams is a great pop idol. You get everything with him: controversy; great quotes; he's had success and failure. His personal life has been up and down as well. The British public specially like people who've been there, lost it all, then come back again. Kylie is good too.

**Dec:** I agree.

*How would you advise the contestants to cope with fame?*

**Ant:** The main thing is to enjoy yourself.

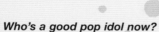

*But you can enjoy yourself being a diva and ordering everyone around.*

**Dec:** If that's what it takes, hahah! Be yourself. It's a fantastic opportunity that not many people will get. I don't think you should ever forget how lucky you are.

**Ant:** You can very quickly become cynical about it, because you can suddenly see the other side of the music industry. Try not to let that happen.

**Dec:** You never know what's going to happen tomorrow. People could stop buying your records, or you could leave your house and get hit by a bus. So enjoy every day. Some days are harder than others. You might have photographers following you, that's all part and parcel of what you're doing, but don't …

**Ant:** … whinge.

## KATE THORNTON: Pop Idol Extra Presenter

*What qualities do you need to be the Pop Idol?*

Performance; vocals; good songs; star quality.

### Who's a good Pop Idol now?

The US is shaming Britain with pop acts. The benchmarks are Christina Aguilera, Justin Timberlake, Beyoncé. I think Beyoncé nails it on every level: she's an amazing songwriter, producer, arranger. She pulls it off live; she looks great; she's smart and focussed.

### How would you advise the contestants to cope with fame?

It will be like a tidal wave when it hits them. I find it terrifying. I wouldn't be able to handle what's coming to them. If they stay focussed and treat it with a sense of humour, then it will be OK. Will Young is a smart guy, a good egg. He can step back and see it for what it is. Even then, Will struggled sometimes. But he loves singing, even though he doesn't love being famous.

## JOHN AND CE CE: Pop Idol Vocal Coaches

### What qualities do you need to be the Pop Idol?

**John:** What I loved about Will Young was that the minute he got on stage, you could see he enjoyed himself there. He shone; he has a natural charisma.

**Ce Ce:** You have to enjoy it, not look like you're facing the flying squad. You have to have a voice which, when you turn on the radio and hear it, is instantly recognisable.

### Who's a good Pop Idol now?

**John:** Will Young. He drives his own car, he'd make you a cup of tea, he's the sort of role model we need. He's not rude to others, he's no diva.

### How would you advise the contestants to cope with fame?

**Ce Ce:** To know that not everyone will like you – it would be boring if we were all the same.

## MADS: Pop Idol Stylist

### Who's a good Pop Idol now?

Gwen Stefani from No Doubt, Robbie Williams … Kylie has gone a bit cheap. Madonna is still great. Christina Aguilera is better.

## SHELLEY: The Pop Idol Press Officer

### What qualities do you need to be the Pop Idol?

The public have to look for someone they can support in the long term, so that they keep buying your records, looking for new stories, new styles. They need a pop idol that will live up to all the pop star expectations whilst remaining the person they have grown to know and love right from the early auditions. You don't necessarily have to be a pop idol – that was shown with Will last year, whose new album is a lot more jazzy. Just as long as you've got the talent, image and personality it doesn't matter what genre of music you decide to make.

### Who's a good Pop Idol now?

I love the old classics: Madonna; George Michael. I like a bit of Busted, Will and Gareth. Rachel Stevens is fantastic.

### How would you advise the contestants to cope with fame?

They haven't had time to adapt, but the papers are building them up every week, making them celebrities, and that will inevitably happen. They need to keep their family and friends close to them. They need to think carefully before they do or say anything that may be brought up or used against them in their future careers. And *without* doing anything, they generate publicity. I also think it's not necessarily a good idea for them to read the papers everyday. A negative piece can have a devastating effect on their performances – the timing's important.

# At Home with the Pop Idols

So who lives in a house like this? There are bottles of champagne in the fridge, trays of sandwiches in the kitchen. A camera flashbulb goes off upstairs; there are clothes everywhere. Freebie bags of hair straighteners have just arrived, and certain people are jumping up and down so that their knees might almost fall off with excitement.

Of course, this is the Pop Idols' house and those 'certain people' are the eight finalists. The mansion in central London is four floors of chaos. Today they have a shoot with *Now* magazine. Yesterday they filmed the video for their Christmas single in Townhouse Studios, along with the rest of the final twelve contestants.

Today is Roxanne's 17th birthday – her first birthday away from home – and she can't stop grinning. Her parents are coming round later to take her out. 'I'm so old now,' she laughs. 'I might have to retire.' She goes to get her make-up retouched. Susanne pops into the kitchen to make a cup of tea but is foiled because she has to go upstairs and have another photo done. There's no let up in this game called, er, fame.

The house is huge, and Sam takes us on a guided tour. There's a big lounge on the first floor with swanky telly and big sofas. The other night, says Sam, the girls made them watch *Dirty Dancing* on DVD. And – yes – he didn't think it was all that bad. He's loving it in London and in the house – his first trip to the capital was at the Criterion auditions. 'My parents rang up yesterday and asked whether I was missing them,' he says. 'And I had to say, "Not as much as I thought…" They were quite upset – we're a close family – but I haven't had time to think about home.' Not surprised, really.

The boys' bedrooms are very tidy, but the girls… Ooh, Kim and Roxanne's room is a right mess, let's be frank. There are clothes and jewellery *everywhere*.

'It's not *that* bad,' says Roxie when Sam confronts her.

'Ok, but Kim's a mother,' says Sam, cheekily. 'What's the world coming to?' Kim just throws a look back at Sam.

Andy and Michelle have been up to their old tricks – their ever-escalating practical jokes are ruining everyone's kip. After Michelle got a picture of Andy as a three-year-old, and Dec showed it to the nation live on TV, Andy has been trying to get her back.
He's been attempting to get a picture of her asleep, and so far he's failed – only getting a picture of her hair because he couldn't see anything. But she woke up at 3am the next night and took a picture of him with her bra cup on his head! Good gracious! 'She always goes one step further, it's so annoying,' says Andy.

It's plain to see that they absolutely revel in each other's company, and lurve being in the swank pad. At six, Roxanne's parents arrive to go out for a meal. Later, Susanne takes some of the older Pop Idollers out to the local pub. 'I picked one I thought they wouldn't recognise us in,' she says. 'But someone did come up to me in the loo…' Remember, once in *Pop Idol*, you cannot escape.

Has anyone ruined anything? Set fire to the sofa? Vomited on the carpet?

'I nearly set fire to the wok,' says Sam, who was cooking a stir-fry for everyone. 'Oh, and I spilt coffee on my bed.'

'It looks like a wee stain,' adds Roxanne, and thus a great debate commences, with Mark joining in, about whether Sam is safer admitting to the production crew that he 'wee-ed' in his bed or spilt coffee – these Pop Idols are a very silly bunch, sometimes.

It's big. It's on another scale altogether. And it's terrifying.

It's the start of *Pop Idol* proper, where twelve go down to two… and those two fight it out to be crowned the nation's Pop Idol 2003.

Blimey!

And no wonder there has been some wobblers. Seeing the set for the first time at rehearsals during the week, some of the twelve have been a little overawed at the size of the studio, and the *realness* of the competition – the set looks a lot smaller on TV. Susanne did a bit of blubbing on Thursday, Kim on Friday morning.

The set is the well-known metally construction from the first series, made from a combination of the insides of old washing machines and industrial cheese graters*, and it has not been sitting in a storeroom since Will Young became the UK's first *Pop Idol* winner in February 2002. It was shipped over to Holland for the Dutch *Pop Idol* then shipped back. There's some new neon lights and back lighting, to make it all the more impressive. There's still the mesh stairs that everyone's worried their high heels will get caught in (even the girls).

The atmosphere this week, however, is not all fear. The twelve are getting on famously; they're a raucous bunch. Brian and Mark are the jokers; Kim (a real mummy to her three kids) is the mummy of the group. Even little Leon is coming out of his shell, although he has had root-canal treatment on his teeth this week. Ouch. They're still nervous about Saturday, but, according to the singing teachers, they've all upped their game. 'Emotions are high,' says John on Friday. 'Nerves are getting to them, but they're sounding good.'

By the end of Friday afternoon, Ce Ce muses on her and John's role as vocal coaches. 'We don't teach, we *diagnose*,' she laughs. 'There's a lot of baggage, they've been told some bad things in the past, we help iron out things. A handful of them here are brilliant singers, though.'

Michelle, however, has spent three days in bed. She lost her voice while she was ill. She's not sure how good her singing will be. 'Five weeks in which I could have got the flu and I get it on *Tuesday*!' she says in the studio canteen. She hasn't eaten for two days, so has a salad. She's determined to perform; she's not going to sit the week out, that's for losers. 'This is my big chance,' she continues. 'I've not warmed up and I've not had any vocal training, but I don't want to blow it. There's no way I'm pulling out tomorrow night, I don't want a week's grace, I'm here and I wanna do it.'

John and Ce Ce watch rehearsals from the judges' desk, and make notes. There's a rail of clothes by the side of the set: this week the contestants wear their own garb, and next week stylist Mads will bring them the finest garments known to humanity. (Fair to say they're all quite excited about this.)

Ant and Dec are wandering around, ready to start rehearsals. 'I've been reading the first few chapters of the book,' says Dec, who sees the copy before it goes to print. 'It's a real page turner!' He's excited about being back on the set – the last time he was here was in 2002 when Will Young scooped the title. He says of this year's twelve: 'This is where it starts to get really exciting; it's what we've all been waiting for. It's nice to be back. But we've got twelve completely different characters, it will be interesting to see how they gel, work together and fight against each other. These big shows separate the wheat from the chaff, it's all quite nerve wracking.'

Showtime. (Let's not mention nerves again, shall we?) And have the judges transformed into lovely, cuddly persons of praise and congratulation? Er, not really.

## The Judges' Verdict

According to Pete, Nicki, Simon and Foxy, Kirsty and Leon will find it 'tough' to get through this week; Mark is taking a 'risk' singing U2; Michelle is 'boring'; Chris still looks like a vicar (he *hates* that); and Roxanne is told she must 'learn to be cool again'. But Susanne is 'sensational'; Kim is 'sassy'; and Marc is 'special'. Sam has 'real presence'; both Andy and Brian are 'brilliant'… but Brian is 'forgettable' too (eh?). Phew.

And so for the next hour while the viewers vote their brains out, all twelve are teetering on the edge of madness. This time, there's no second chance. It's a cruel sport, but part of showbiz.

After about 30 minutes, the suits who know how the voting is going *still* find it impossible to gauge who's going out this week: the bottom six are changing all the time. This fact doesn't help the contestants much. Roxanne is upset about the judges' comments (she's had a little cry), as is Michelle who tries not to show it. Kirsty feels that because she went first, people might have forgotten her. But Susanne is happy; Marc is happy (the judges loved him); Kim is extremely happy – it's her boyfriend who's more nervous than she is...

Will Young, who was pretty good last year, comes along to wish everyone well. He says he finds it odd being at the studio – and it's making him nervous too. He wishes luck to all the contestants who are indeed very starstruck to see him there.

Now – gasp – it's the results. The dreaded old awful old results. (But it wouldn't be the show without them, friends.) Even Ant and Dec don't know how the voting is going until the last moment. Even before they're announced, the twelve all look very upset; some look like they're holding back the tears already. In fact, they *all* look like they've just had root canal treatment. And Bah! Leon and Kirsty have the lowest votes, so they are going home tonight. And

Kirsty is all tears, bless her – she really didn't expect it. Leon is sanguine, and Nicki Chapman tries to cheer him up by saying what a tremendous voice he has. He just hopes that someone will see him on the show and make him a star. He looks very calm about the whole thing.

But the ten left still feel terrible. 'We got on so well,' says Sam. 'It's hard to see two people go…' Mark R agrees – they really do love each other, this bunch. 'I didn't perform as well as these guys,' he sniffs. 'Kirsty was brilliant, Leon as well. You're up on a high, then you feel like someone has just punched you in the ribs.'

Ant, Dec and Kate Thornton are in complete shock too. 'It is so upsetting,' says Ant. 'I forgot how hard it hits you, having to go through the results show. We came so far with them…'

Simon wanders up to where they are standing. His attitude is: toughen up, young presenters. 'Two people went, and of course they're going to go,' he states. 'We're not giving twelve people a record contract, if we didn't kick anyone out nobody would watch the show.'

Harsh, but right, although Lovely Nicki is on hand to comfort Leon and Kirsty because they both need it. And what's worse? The

horrors continue next week when two more contestants get the boot… Argh! It *is* worse than root-canal treatment. But a lot more interesting and entertaining and downright marvellous to watch.

* Probably.

---

**Brian Ormond**
'A Different Corner' (George Michael)

**Michelle McManus**
'All By Myself' (Celine Dion)

**Chris Hide**
Don't Let the Sun Go Down On Me'
(Elton John)

**Leon McPherson**
'I Just Called To Say I Love You'
(Stevie Wonder)

**Andy Scott-Lee**
'If You're Not the One' (Daniel Bedingfield)

**Kirsty Crawford**
'I'm Outta Love' (Anastacia)

**Kim Gee**
'River Deep Mountain High' (Tina Turner)

**Roxanne Murphy**
'Still the One' (Shania Twain)

**Marc Dillon**
'To Love Somebody' (Michael Bolton)

**Mark Rhodes**
'With Or Without You' (U2)

**Susanne Manning**
'Ironic' (Alanis Morrissette)

**Sam Nixon**
Handbags and Gladrags' (Rod Stewart)

Once upon a time, one Hallowe'en, there was a TV studio. It was very quiet: the canteen persons were calmly cooking baked potatoes; the crew were slurping cups of tea. A hush was upon the Fountain Studios, for ten young talented contestants had not yet arrived.

But when they did appear – what noise, what chatter! Brian is carrying his Scary Movie mask – he says he scared the living daylights out of Michelle this morning. They've all just moved to a luxury swank pad, in a secret location in central London, and they're loving it. Chris is very excited about all the stairs. 'You don't need to go to the gym, you get fit by running up and down all the time.' Sam has been cooking for them in the house. Roxanne is enthused, 'He made us a lovely meal: soup, chicken, it was all really nice. It's been brilliant. I don't want to go home.'

Everyone has lunch, although Mark, Marc, Brian and Andy have to be dragged away from the table footie to eat. It's all very pally – everyone looks like they've forgotten it's a competition, that the fight is on. The girls sit around the table with Kate Thornton and talk girly matters - underwear, things like that. Kim and Michelle are in high spirits today. Yesterday they were given free clothes from a high street store. And Kim is especially pleased, because she's also had a nice hair-do by Nicki Chapman's hairdresser Richard Ward. Kim's kids were down in London yesterday – they went on the tube for the first time and Milly nearly got left behind at one station! They were thrilled to be in the capital, and kept asking their mum, 'Are we at *Pop Idol* yet?'

And more excitement: Sam is baking today. As soon as he's finished his lunch, he's off to the kitchen canteen to make a chocolate cake. He never stops, does he? But no one can have a piece until it is properly cooked. 'Go Sam!' shouts Kate Thornton. 'Go Sam!' shout the crew. And, indeed, off he goes… to the oven.

This week the Pop Idollers have been busy doing more than urging Sam to cook them fine foods. They've spent the last few days recording their Christmas single and album. It was the first time in the studio for all of them except Andy, who isn't Pop Star Jaded at all, and says it was great. Everyone is so darned positive! They actually – really really truly – are positive, if that's a proper sentence. It's very refreshing; if you like positive young hopefuls with breeches full of talent. And we all do.

'Oh my goodness!' 'Aw!' 'Look!' What is this all about? Sam, spying his newly baked cake? Marc watching himself blubbing on the telly again? No! It's the girls who've just stepped into stylist Mads' wardrobe room and spotted…

Shoes.

There are heaps of them. All very girly, pointy, booty, high heels, pumps. Susanne is in heaven, 'They're so gorgeous!' Roxanne is delighted. Oh, they all are. Mads is a very popular man this afternoon.

'I've been shopping like a madman,' he says. 'I've been to shops, showrooms, press offices. I did ten hours of shopping on Monday and Tuesday.'

Apparently, another stylist on Channel Four was rude about Mads, because he's dressed everyone down thus far. 'I don't want to hit too hard,' he says, scowling. 'I'm not going to glam everyone up until we get closer to the finale.' Quite right. And there are no dubious tank tops on the hangers this year – hoorah for Mads and his style.

The contestants warm up with the singing teachers and do a quick rehearsal. 'I think it's easier this week,' says Susanne, 'because we've done one show. But it's not going to be any easier saying goodbye if we go out.' Everyone nods. They know that Saturday is the best day – they perform songs they love – but also the worst. They could be chucked out.

On Saturday, nerves again are high, like pylons. The worst bit, it seems, is the standing in the wings for each contestant, waiting to go on. That booming *Pop Idol* music, the hungry audience, the evil smirks of the judges…

Hayley Evetts is in the audience tonight and she admits afterwards that she is terrified for each of the ten. 'I've been there! I know exactly what it feels like!' she says. She also reveals that Will Young phoned her after his visit last week, to warn her how nervous she'd feel – neither of them had been back to the Fountain Studios since.

## The Judges' Verdict

The judges are in fine form – the competition is, naturally, hotting up but it's still so difficult to predict who we'll see in the final. And true enough, performances vary from week to week.

And how do our ten fare? Ooooh, Simon says he's really disappointed this week. Marc's 'Celebrate' 'wasn't a celebration', Kim is 'falling into the karaoke vein', Chris is 'awkward', they can't hear Susanne, Brian is 'pub singer-ish', and Mark R is only 'good enough'. But here's the good news: Andy (who's brought his girlfriend Michelle Heaton tonight) is 'excellent' and Michelle is 'great', while Roxanne is 'a future pop star in the making'.

All ruminate on their comments backstage in the green room as the voting starts. Brian's mum is downstairs, and she has no idea whether he'll go through, all she knows is she's very proud of him. The parents are invited down each week, and for those who live far away, the expense of travelling is worth every penny. Those Pop Idols need support! And t-shirts with their faces printed on, and banners – the works. Have you noticed how Andy always grins at his mum when he's finished his song?

Even those who got great comments are modest after their performance. Andy,

whom all four of the judges adored this week, swears he 'must be dreaming'. Roxanne just grins. Marc D, like vocal lady Ce Ce has said, knows singers have their 'off weeks'. He's just a bit worried that's all. Having an off week in the final ten is a bit… risky.

The results come through. Again, the bottom four have been swapping places all evening – tonight only 8% separates the four, which means it's as close as a whisker. Brian, Kim and Marc make up the bottom three… and Brian and Marc are going home tonight – but there's barely a sniff from ever-blubbing Marc.

Kate has the dreadful task of talking to the contestants after the results, when they're all gloomy. She says she doesn't try and gee them up, 'People are tuning in to see how they're reacting, so I let them set the mood and we don't pretend that they aren't feeling bad.' Nicki, again, is on hand to talk to everyone, as Pop Counsellor. Next week only one goes, but it doesn't make it any easier…

> **Songs from the year they were born – what they sang:**
>
> **Chris**
> 'Heaven' (Bryan Adams)
>
> **Susanne**
> 'Only You' (Yazoo)
>
> **Marc D**
> 'Celebrate' (Kool and the Gang)
>
> **Kim**
> 'Hot Stuff' (Donna Summer)
>
> **Mark R**
> 'Imagine' (John Lennon)
>
> **Brian**
> 'Honesty' (Billy Joel)
>
> **Roxanne**
> 'Take My Breath Away' (Berlin)
>
> **Michelle**
> 'On My Radio' (Donna Summer)
>
> **Andy**
> 'She's Out Of My Life' (Michael Jackson)
>
> **Sam**
> 'True Colours' (Cyndi Lauper)

This week, everybody met Sir Elton John – and had to sing in front of him. Apparently, he was very bling bling – a large ruby ring on his finger impressed everybody. They still can't quite believe they met him. "It's been currazy," says Chris, whose mouth popped open and couldn't quite close as soon as he spotted the singer. "And write that – currazy." They say they could see he was a proper pop star 'cos he wore his shades inside.

They're all back at the Fountain Studios on Friday for rehearsals. The girls talk in their dressing room about the moment they go on stage on Saturday. Kim, especially, is nervous about tomorrow because she was in the bottom three last week.

'It knocked me for six,' she says. 'It's been quite hard, but you have to pick yourself up.'

Do they see the judges before the show?

'I saw Simon in make-up last week,' says Michelle. 'And he came down to the video shoot. It's the first time I've ever had a conversation with him – but he didn't make any eye contact.'

The judges have to distance themselves from the contestants, it seems, in order to preside over events properly. And there's been a right old hoo-ha in the papers about certain MPs wanting to table a motion to protect kids from Simon Cowell and his terrible band of judges, or something. They feel that youngsters could be damaged by their comments, especially the more big-boned youngsters … and this is all when Simon has stood up for Michelle from day one! The judges are furious. Nicki says she thinks it's 'frustrating when people interfere with something they don't know about'. Pete agrees: 'We do our job,' he says. 'And they don't do theirs.'

Kim, Michelle and Susanne are more concerned with doing their job. That one where you have to sing in front of a few million people, live every Saturday night. That terrifying, crucifying experience. Yeah, that's the one.

'John and Ce Ce tell you what to do all week,' says Michelle. 'But your bottle crashes when you're waiting to go on. You just have to open your mouth and hope for the best.'

'At the dress-rehearsal last week I forgot my words,' adds Susanne. 'Now, all I'm thinking is, don't forget the words! It's something just to manage to sing the song and not stop in the middle.'

And what is so terrifying?

'Oh, it's the lighting,' says Michelle, looking really quite worried already. 'And when you hear them say your name. I know I'm OK if I've sung the first line without shaking too much.'

## The Judges' Verdict

This week is a bit of a winner. The audience go loopy for the performances; the judges think it's a much better show tonight. In the spooky starter slot (they're all terrified of being first) is Roxanne, and the judges think she's 'brilliant'. Andy is 'bloody brilliant', no less, and Simon tells Michelle that, as a fan and not a judge, he loves her. Cor. Sam is 'every inch a young pop star' and Mark is 'bloody good'. Yet Susanne is branded a 'musical train wreck', Chris is 'absolutely terrible' and Kim is good, but chose a very hard song that few people knew.

After the show, the high from being on stage doesn't last as long as you'd think. 'You get the adrenalin for about five minutes after you've performed,' says Kim. 'But then it drops, and you're tired.'

Within 15 minutes from the start of voting, tonight is already the biggest vote ever. Elton has been on the phone from LA, wondering how everyone did, and asking someone to ring him with the results. None

of our eight look very cheered by this – they're still on tenterhooks, and will be dangling for quite a while.

It's the closest vote ever – only 9% separates everyone. It's a shocker – Kim, Roxanne and Michelle are in the bottom three. The judges predicted Kim and Chris would certainly be there, but are dumbfounded that Roxie is… She starts crying, and they all look like they're going to blub. Everyone looks like a train has crashed into the studio.

It's Kim who's going home this week. 'When I saw that Roxanne and Michelle were there too, I knew it was me,' she says. 'Kim has shown how you can look different, I think she's fantastic,' says Nicki after the show. Kim is emotional but still supports her Pop Idol pals. 'Every single one of them deserves to win,' she says.

But only one will…

---

**What they sang… Sir Elton's songs…**
*(and not forgetting Bernie Taupin who wrote the words, and Tim Rice)*

**Chris** - *Circle of Life'*

**Kim** - *'The One'*

**Mark** - *'Something About The Way You Look Tonight'*

**Michelle** - *'Your Song'*

**Andy** - *'Can You Feel The Love Tonight'*

**Roxanne** - *'Sorry Seems to Be the Hardest Word'*

**Susanne** - *'I Guess That's Why they Call It The Blues'*

**Sam** - *'I Want Love'*

## Alton Towers

'Aaaaaaaaaaaaaaaaaaaaaaaargh!'

It's a cold, misty Monday morning, but the Pop Idols are having a whale of a time. We're in Alton Towers, and they are going on the most nail-biting rides that they can manage. They're also joined by kids from the Make A Wish Foundation, who are thrilled to meet the magnificent seven.

'I definitely think that Sam has been the bravest today,' says Andy afterwards in the Alton Towers hotel. 'I think he's done extremely well.'

'I've been really brave as well,' pipes up Roxanne. 'I was scared, I thought I was going to be sick everywhere. I don't like big fast rides like that. Oblivion topped it off for me; it was horrible. I'm never going to go on it again.'

'I'm just surprised my breakfast didn't reappear,' laughs Susanne.

Is it good to get away and forget about Saturday?

'Yeah,' says Roxanne. 'You've always got to have that bit of fun.'

'The week goes so quick,' says Andy. 'Before you know it, it's Saturday. It relieves the stress, I think, going on the rides.'

The kids have provided an inspiration.

'It made us all realise how lucky we are,' says Sam (who's still feeling queasy from the rides). 'You see how much they love life. It was amazing. They were full of energy.'
'We were all petrified of the rides, to be honest,' says Mark. 'But the kids were saying, "Come On!"' Mark has just met someone who lives on his street, a few doors down from him. 'I'm a bit freaked out,' he says.

The contestants have had a 'brilliant' day. 'It could almost rival meeting Elton John,' says Susanne. They go back to their rooms to chill out then have dinner. Some are absolutely exhausted, and retire to bed early, while hardier types Mark, Sam and Michelle find it easier to stay up and enjoy 'refreshments' with the production team…

Back from Alton Towers, our magnificent seven have work to do. They have picked their songs and go into the studio as soon as they get to London to record their backing tracks. This week the theme is Disco, and a few are considerably worried. Disco tunes are hard to sing; Marc Dillon found this when he sang 'Celebration' and got kicked off. Susanne knows it's not her genre; Chris is also worried. They're further confused by last week's shock bottom three – anyone could go this week, depending on the whims of the audience at home.

Ce Ce and John think it's going to be a hard week. 'It's a shame that it can't just be a fun week but the judges will be scrutinising their every move,' says John. 'They just have to give it 100% and the judges won't be able to argue with that.'

Although the contestants have been told a little boogie-ing won't go amiss, there is no choreographer on hand. 'We tell them where the camera will be, and at what point in the song,' says Ce Ce. 'And they can go through some movements if they want to.'

The crowd are good at geeing up the singers, but the crucial difference between what the studio audience and viewers at home see, is the sound level.

'The backing track is quite high in the studio,' says Ce Ce. 'But the vocals are mixed louder on the TV. That's why Simon couldn't hear Susanne last week, but she sounded fine.'

Michelle is not too concerned – her voice suits the style – but she has the added distraction of a pair of diamond earrings, which her fan Mark (who first sent her a bunch of flowers) has sent her. (Needless to say, she hasn't phoned him yet.)

On Saturday night it's a packed show: Kelly Clarkson makes an appearance, singing her latest single and giving the contestants advice. (In *American Idol* the finalists had to wait a day for the results, not a couple of hours.)

Some of the finalists struggle, some sail through – but this time none of them are sure who might be in the bottom three, it's down to the very unpredictable votes from the Public.

## The Judges' Verdict

Susanne goes first (yikes, etc.) and the judges veer from calling her 'unique' to 'awful'. Andy, too, is both 'marvellous' and 'mediocre'. Mark is 'fantastic' and 'cabaret'. ?? But Michelle gets a whole-hearted response – Simon just saying 'I loved it'. Roxanne looks like she's 'been performing for years' and Sam 'sets the standard' tonight. Lastly, the judges call Chris's rendition of 'Ain't Nobody' 'peculiar': nothing more than that. And, if the *Official Pop Idol Book* can be frank here, it is very odd indeed.

Ricky Gervais is in the audience tonight (NB See the series one *Pop Idol Official Book* for

our brush with him at the final last year) and he's very enthusiastic about the show. 'It's fantastic!' he gurgles. 'It's probably better than last year. If I go out on Saturdays, I tape it. It's a treat.'

But does he vote?

'I don't vote at the general election so I'm not going to vote on *Pop Idol*. Andy and Roxanne are the best pop packages, but I like Susanne. She wasn't as good tonight and she knew that. Am I a nerd to be talking like this?'

Of course not! Everyone should be talking like this. But we have to fly off and listen to the dreaded result.

Jaws wobble, eyes get teary, noses drip. The bottom two this week are Susanne and Andy (although the judges name Roxanne and Chris). Although Susie is sure she's off, it's Andy who's told he has to pack his bags. Awks! He was the bookies' number one favourite* – another shocker! That's it, there're tears from everyone. Well, almost everyone.

'As cruel as it sounds,' says Simon, 'this is a winner's competition. So you lose the competition, you go, who cares? The focus has to be on the winner.'

A voice rings out from the studio audience, 'What about Gareth, then?'

It's cheeky Michelle, Andy's girlfriend. She raises a good point. Mr Gates came second and got a record deal. She and her bandmates from Liberty X didn't win *PopStars*, but have had a longer and more credible career than Hear'Say.

'Well, I have the right to change my mind, next week,' says the head judge. Ooh Simon, you are awful.

Pete is just amazed by how the Public changes its collective mind every week – this is totally unlike the first series where Will, Gareth and Darius had loyal fans from early on.

Foxy thinks Andy will do well, and Nicki is on hand, as ever, to wish Andy the best of luck, and keep his confidence up.
'Andy did not give the weakest performance tonight,' she says. 'It's a big world out there,' says Nicki, knowing that a record label could well spot him and sign him up. 'People have got to remember he has become so much better from the first time we saw him, to now. And he's a great bloke.'

And that's important.

*\* Something to do with the terrible world of gambling.*

**Mark**
'More Than A Woman' *(The Bee Gees)*

**Michelle**
'If I Can't Have You' *(Yvonne Elliman)*

**Andy**
'Rock With You' *(Jackson 5)*

**Roxanne**
Can You Feel It' *(Jackson 5)*

**Susanne**
'Young Hearts Run Free' *(Candi Staton)*

**Sam**
'Blame It On The Boogie' *(Jackson 5)*

**Chris**
'Ain't Nobody' *(Chaka Khan)*

## At Home With The Pop Idols... Again

What strikes you when visiting the house again is the security and privacy. Each window pane is covered with an opaque film, which lets in light but means no evil paparazzi can snap the Pop Idols when they're cart wheeling or picking their nose (perish the thought).

There's a big entry phone and electronic gates. There is no telephone here – everyone uses mobiles. At one point, Michelle's mobile rings when she's out and Susanne is cautious and won't answer it: 'The number isn't coming up as a name, so it might not be someone she knows'. The Tabloids could be anywhere. Phoning up, or dressed as a tree outside. (Turns out the missed call was Michelle's sister who was at work.)

Thursday is a quiet day for the Pop Idols. This week they've filmed the ad for their Christmas album, they've had a big magazine photo shoot, they've had to record their Big Band song early – because it's with live instruments – and they've been to the gym. Phew. 'My legs ache,' says Michelle, who – at 11am – is making her breakfast (microwaved bacon sarnie – as part of her low fat diet). 'But I enjoyed it. I go swimming three times a week so it wasn't too bad for me.'

Oh, and how could we forget? The Pop Idols went to the premiere of *Love Actually* on Monday. And they loved it, actually. Haw. 'It was great,' says Susanne. 'There was Alan Rickman, who I love. He watches the show. Isn't that weird?'

'Hugh Grant didn't know who we were,' says Roxanne. 'He looked a bit frightened of us lot.'

Michelle met Colin Firth, whom she adores. She even has a cutout of him in her Glasgow flat. She went wobbly for ages. Best bit of all,

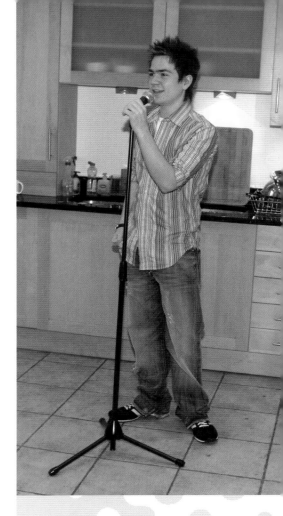

however, was a chocolate fountain, which was a big hit with everyone. 'And it was quality chocolate, too,' mentions Susanne. That's important.

And they say this is a quiet day. Sam comes back from rehearsing his song, just has time to chomp on a sandwich when a new microphone stand is delivered to the house so he can practise for Saturday. He starts straightaway, in the kitchen. He's thrilled to be singing a Beatles song; he has every album and loves them to bits. This is the week when he can truly be Sam, he reckons.

Mark's busy upstairs in the living room with Ce Ce and John, who are going through 'Help' with him. He's having fun doing the falsetto bits. Little does he know that when he goes for a facial and a sun bed session later this afternoon, those falsetto notes will be easier to reach. Mark doesn't realise you leave your boxers *on* when you go on the sun bed. Ouch.

# Ant and Dec tell us a thing or two

On Friday at the Fountain Studios, the award-winning* Ant and Dec are milling around the café. They carry a big burden – not only do they have to look those fearsome judges in the eye every week, but they have to give the contestants the results. The worst job in showbiz? Perhaps. They get an indication of the results about half an hour before they're announced, and are told in the break, when the lines are closed, who will be going home.

'When it's so close, they tell us in our ear when we're live on stage,' says Ant, referring to the weeny earpieces live TV presenters wear, so they can be told things nicely by the series producers in the gallery. 'The week Leon went out, our series producer, Claire Horton, didn't think we'd heard what she'd said. We said, 'The person going home this week is…' and I'd kept a nice gap, for dramatic effect. Claire says in my ear, "Leon!" Then all we hear is, "Leon Leon *Leon*! It's *Leon*!"'

It must be hard to look the contestants in the eye when you know who's going out… 'It is difficult,' says Dec. 'But we manage.' Do you ever expect to be slapped by an angry finalist when they hear the news?

'Oh no,' says Ant. 'It's like, we're just passing a message on… Don't shoot the messenger, mate. It wasn't us who did it! It's the public!'

The only person who sees who tops the votes each week is executive producer Richard Holloway. Claire Horton is only told what she needs to know for the results show.

On Saturday night the vocal coaches are really geared up. 'I'm really excited about this week,' says Ce Ce. 'If anyone struggles I think Michelle might, because she's a mezzo soprano singing a Beatles track and

we had to change the key.'
'I think it's hard this week to see who's going to go,' says John.

Do the coaches have favourites?
'I can honestly say,' says Ce Ce. 'That when I first started with the final 12 I really thought I would. But I don't, because they're so different. There's no two people who I see fitting in the same genre, they're not alike at all.'

What about the ruddy Public and their shock voting tactics? No one knows who's going out.

'It's exciting but we have no idea either. I don't think anyone, even the judges, have a clue. No one would have guessed Andy was going to leave last week. I just hope that the people picking up the phones are the people who are going to go out and buy the records. That is very important.'

But Douglas, the glossy-haired pianist, has doubts about this. 'I don't think they *are* going to buy the records,' he says. 'The viewers are still voting for personality, for the underdogs. They're still strongly influenced by people who are given a hard time.'

It's a funny one. But onto the show, which is a lot stronger than last week, to be frank; and has the studio crowd going nuts-a-mental.

## The Judges' Verdict

Sam is '****** awesome', Susanne is 'back' after 'three quite duff weeks' and Chris makes Pete cry. Which makes Chris cry too. Aw. Roxanne gets a mixed reception, which makes her upset, and Mark is told he's a bit karaoke. But again, it's Michelle that has Simon frothing at the mouth. 'I'm so bored of the same look over and over again. You bring a breath of fresh air to the competition, and a breath of fresh air to pop music.' Bloomin' Nora. He's smitten, that lad.

The public votes. And they vote again. In fact, over one million votes are cast, a record so far in this series. But again – it's a complete shocker. All the judges reckon Mark will be going home tonight … and it's Roxanne! Blub! And blub again!

'I thought I'd see her in the final three,' says Nicki Chapman. 'And I haven't said that about anyone so far. I truly believe that if Roxanne worked with a good producer and got her range right, she'd be a huge pop star.'

Time will tell.

* Triple winners again at the National Television Awards this year. Hoorah.

---

**What they sang… Beatle's songs…**

**Mark** - 'Help'

**Michelle** - 'Hey Jude'

**Roxanne** - 'Let It Be'

**Susanne** - 'Ticket To Ride'

**Sam** - 'With A Little Help From My friends'

**Chris** - 'The Long And Winding Road'

Controversy. It makes the world go round, a little bit like money… and music. And on a show like *Pop Idol* controversy (*and* music… *and* money) is never far away. The 'news'papers are hungry for *Pop Idol* gossip. And when there isn't any, they just, er, make it up.

This week has seen the press frothing at the mouth, claiming that Michelle asnd Susanne have had a 'blazing' row. They report that Susanne called Michelle a 'fat cow'. And is it true?
'Nonsense, nonsense, nonsense!' says Susanne.
'Complete and utter rubbish,' says Michelle, both girls in the Fountain Studios for rehearsal day. The story broke when the contestants had a few days off, and weren't in the *Pop Idol* Mansion together. Michelle was initially hurt. 'I woke up in the morning thinking, "Oh, Susanne thinks I'm a fat cow. That's fantastic,"' she says.

'I was making breakfast,' says Susanne. 'Someone rang and said, "Have you seen today's papers?" I hadn't seen it, but I was told all these quotes that supposedly I said. Those are the things people said to *me* when I was growing up. I'm the last person in the world to say those things to someone else.'

Susanne rang Michelle and cleared it up immediately. Perhaps it's the papers taking up Pete's accusation last week that the finalists were all too close, and not hungry for it. They've invented a story which shows there's some real rivalry.

The Pop Idollers all enjoyed going home for a few days. It was very good but it was also very strange. *We* all know they're famous, but they still find it hard to get it into their heads.  Funny really. You'd think they would have an inkling by now.

'Going home made us all realise how big the show is,' says Sam, sitting in the dressing room. 'You can't go out without being recognised, you can't still be normal, like.'

Sam did a gig in the local shopping centre and over 2,000 fans turned up. He's still in shock. Re-bespectacled Chris (ie he's got his glasses back on) went home and says the phone rang a lot and his dad spent all day watching the shows back. He went to his old school and was mobbed, so much so that some youngsters pinned him against the wall in their bid for autographs.

'I had a wicked time when I went home,' says Michelle, having a curly hair day. 'I went out with all my friends in Shawlands, Glasgow. Someone actually paid for my dinner for me. I was sitting there having a meal with friends, and a guy came up and said, "I'll pay for your bill." You don't realise the impact that *Pop Idol* makes. 'Cos we're down here in this wee bubble.'

Susanne was spotted in her local coffee shop. 'It was great going back to normal, well, sort of normal,' she says. She was nabbed by fans, and someone asked her to record an answer phone message for him on his phone. A little more bizarre, she has been asked to present Playboy TV. Probably, with very few clothes on. 'But the guys at 19 Management do such a good job of shielding us from everything,' she says. 'Like offers from Playboy and keeping us away from the press. That's why they start making things up. It's hurtful, because you think, who is saying things about me? You get paranoid.'

Similar things happened last series, when there was a story about Will and Gareth's parents hating each other. The story was a complete fabrication but everyone still got upset.

Of course, it's Big Band week this week. All five contestants are chuffed they're able to sing with a live band.

'Big Band was the reason why I entered *Pop Idol*,' says Michelle, who was sick before she went on stage last Saturday. 'I've never sung anything on this scale before. Up to this point I didn't think that I had a chance of winning the competition. Now we're in the final five, any one of us could win. Last week I thought, we're only a few

weeks away from finding out who's going to win this competition, and whose life is going to change forever. So that's why I vomited.'

On Saturday the contestants are revved up, and there are people with violin cases everywhere, banging into things. It's a bit like *Some Like It Hot*. John and Ce Ce want them to do well, but 'they've got to carry the song, the musicians can't do it for them.' The judges are looking forward to this. The competition goes up a level.

## The Judges' Verdict

Michelle is first on. She looks like a diva in a sparkly cape, but you can see she's watching her heels as she steps down the metal stairs. 'You put your stamp on the competition, you're saying I deserve to be here and I could win this' says her new admirer, Mr Simon Cowell.

Chris, who looks like an odd cross between a dentist and Morrissey, absolutely shines. As Foxy says, 'The vicar just got slicker'.

Susanne wears a 1950s style dress and looks like Marilyn Monroe, as she gives an emotive performance. Nicki says she looks 'absolutely stunning up there' but Simon admits 'it didn't quite do it for me.'

Mark gives his cheeky grin and looks very much the sparkly-eyed crooner. Foxy, er, calls him a 'yummy Brummie'.

Sam, finally, looks like a lovely hedgehog in a dinner jacket. Pete says, 'One word: winner' and Simon tells him 'You've booked your place in the final.'

After the show the judges, well, hmm… they look a little disappointed, left a little cold by the whole event. And indeed, Simon admits 'I'm not jumping out of my chair' with excitement. Pete, too, says of the contestant's choices 'it's not what *they* like, it's what the public likes.' But the public loved this – they're getting the biggest volume of votes this series. So there.

What's clear is again, the bottom two are close – there's only 1% in it. But this week the finalists are much more chipper after their performances. They are not looking as suicidal as in previous weeks.

'With people playing instruments it seemed as though it was halving the pressure on us,' says Mark. 'This time, everyone got good comments. You shouldn't mind if you do go tonight.'

Wise words, mate. And when the votes are counted and someone has to leave tonight, it's between Mark and Susanne. And someone *looks* like she knows she's out… bless her. Not a tear in sight as Susanne hugs her friends goodbye and exudes an air of immense relief.

'I did think I was going, you just know these things,' she says afterwards. 'Everyone else raised their game. I've no problem going out this week, I can hold my head up with that performance … and I'm wearing a great dress.'

### What they sang…

**Mark**
**'Miss Jones'** (Frank Sinatra)

**Susanne**
**'Cry Me A River'** (Julie London)

**Sam**
**'Mr Bojangles'** (Sammy Davis Jnr)

**Michelle**
**'Feeling Good'** (Nina Simone)

**Chris**
**'Ain't That A Kick In The Head'**
(Frank Sinatra)

# Week 7

## Four become three

Christmas comes early in *Pop Idol* land. While normal people still have to go to work and things like that, our Pop Idollers are preparing their house with festive decorations. When they can take a break from practising for Saturday's show.

First, up goes the tree. It's about 12' tall and takes ages to decorate. They place their Christmas presents for each other under it, wrapped in pages from London paper the *Evening Standard*. The four eeny-meeny gifts under the gigantic tree look very silly.

Then it's time for Sam to practise cooking the Christmas meal. He asks the others to peel vegetables and prepare sprouts. They're rubbish. Michelle at least admits she can't cook, but she starts on the carrots as if she's shaving a sensitive chin. Mark does quite well on the sprouts (even though he and Michelle don't like them), but Chris – it's like he's never seen a potato peeler before. He can't get a grasp on it at all. 'I've a feeling I'm allergic to potato peelers,' she says. 'Can we have chips instead?' Mark has to help Chris finish the spuds, because it's taking so long.

Sam creates an exciting stuffing for the chicken then asks Chris to help him, er, 'apply' it. 'Treat it like a lady,' says Sam. Chris is, fair to say, a little perturbed by all this.

They put it all in the oven and set the table. There is, it has to be said, a certain 'tumbleweed' effect in the house today. With only four people knocking around the enormous mansion, there's a real sense that we're missing a few people. The dining table looks sparse set for only four.

Back at the studio on Saturday afternoon, it's Christmas too. There are boxes of 'luxury plush gold tip' Santa hats for every audience member, plus crew.

The contestants go through their two songs and then rehearse the judge's comments. Four members of the production crew sit in place of Simon and his 'gang', and make a few remarks. It's all so cool, so laid-back, so easy.

But in actual fact, behind the confident façade, each of the four is panicking. Christmas week is a big worry. Are they going to look cheesy? Are they going to hit the high notes? Now there's four, they can 'smell it', to quote Sam. What he means is one of them is closer than ever to winning the prize, and many are saying this could be anyone's competition, despite the bookies giving Sam the best odds – because the bookies can be wrong (they gave good odds to Andy Scott-Lee…).

Added to this mix are the seven former contestants (Leon has imploded) who are milling around, waiting to rehearse the *Pop Idol* Xmas single performance. They're in two minds about being here, excited to be back on stage, but fearful when they hear that theme music.

In two hours it's showtime, and the final four take to the stage. Michelle sings a Shakin' Stevens song first, for those of you that remember the jelly-legged Welshman. Chris has his trendy specs on, and totally melts the hearts of the audience with 'Winter Wonderland'. Sam rocks to a Wizard tune and Mark grins his way through 'Merry Christmas Everybody'. The next four songs are taken from the *Pop Idol Xmas*

*Factor* album. Michelle sings a serious carol; Mark does Elvis; Sam does a song that Bruce Springsteen also covered, and Chris does the classic 'White Christmas'.

The audience are well in the festive spirit, Michelle's dad got his own round of applause when he walks in. He's dressed as Santa. But are the judges in festive spirit?

|  | **Best comment** | **Worst comment** |
|---|---|---|
| *Mark* | Foxy: *'Thought you did well on the second song'* | Simon: *'Office bloke gets up to sing a song at the Christmas party'* |
| *Sam* | Foxy: *'Millions of girls will want you in their Christmas stocking this year'* | Pete: *'Wasn't your best performance this week'* |
| *Chris* | Nicki: *'Winter Wonderland was awesome'* | Pete: *'No one should ever sing "White Christmas"'* |
| *Michelle* | None | Simon: *'Bloody fantastic!!'* |

The festive four might have got excellent reactions from the judges tonight, but they don't know who's going home tonight. 'I really want to win this,' says Chris who, like the others, has started to become more ambitious. 'This is the worst week ever,' says Sam. 'We just don't know who will be leaving.' Even Michelle is convinced she's for the chop, and she had really good comments.

But when it's time for the judges to predict who will go tonight, they all say Mark. The voting statistics started at between just 3% separating the bottom two, until it's just *1%* in the last five minutes. According to the bigwigs, the lowest-polled singers swapped places during those final moments. Arrrrgh. The tension!

And it's … Chris who's going home tonight. He's absolutely devastated, perhaps the most upset of contestants we've seen so far, and then everyone cries. Boo hoo! Little Chris, to whom his new house mates refer fondly as a 'mentalist' because his brain works in a funny way … Mark says he feels terrible because *he* had psychologically prepared himself to go. Aw.

Chris says afterwards that he didn't even think he'd make final 100, let alone final four. 'I'm not a conventional pop idol, so I've proven that that's not always important…' he sniffs.

'Will Young sent me a text during the show saying Chris was truly amazing,' says Nicki Chapman. 'We all thought he was fantastic tonight… he's an outstanding singer.' You voting public. How unpredictable you are!

**Christmas songs... who sang what...**

*Michelle* *'Merry Christmas Everyone'* & *'Oh Holy Night'*

*Mark* *'Merry Christmas Everybody'* & *'Blue Christmas'*

*Sam* *'I Wish It Could Be Christmas Everyday'* & *'Santa Claus is Coming To Town'*

*Chris* *'Winter Wonderland'* & *'White Christmas'*

## Michelle McManus

**Age: 23**
**From: Glasgow**

### What were you like at school?

I loved school, I had a complete ball. Everyone else my size was bullied, but I liked a laugh with the boys. I went to the football. I was one of the lads. I could take the piss out of myself and I was quite quick off the mark.

### School performances?

My first was as one of the brothers in *Joseph and his Technicolour Dreamcoat*. I was the teacher in *The Boyfriend*. Then I joined the Spotlight Theatre Group and I was the fairy godmother in *Cinderalla* and Rizzo from *Grease*. From 16 I sang in clubs in Glasgow.

### First time you realised you could sing?

My teacher only told me this two weeks ago, but we were singing a hymn in class. I was about eight. I was picked at random to sing solo, and the teacher ran out of the room and told another, 'Have you heard this wee girl sing? You've got to hear it!'

### What's been the best advice you've been given during the show's run?

My dad said, 'Look Michelle, this is what you've wanted to do since you were a wee girl. Enjoy it, remember it's your dream, and what is happening now will affect you for the rest of your life. Don't waste your time. Go and win it!' I've not had that out of my head since I've been here.

### Have you changed since your first audition?

I don't think so, personality-wise. But I always relied on my vocal ability in the past; now I know that's only a third of the package. It's also performance and attitude.

### Who do you think should win?

I couldn't choose, that's too mean.

### What's been the highlight of the show for you?

That moment at the Criterion, which they still show, when I say thanks to Simon because I'm through. That's exactly how it happened, he had to fight to put me through. Pete and Foxy didn't want me in.

*The final three - as seen on their application forms, and as not seen on Pop Idol.*

### Have you had a tantrum yet?

Yeah, in photoshoots. What drives me nuts is the stylists know to buy size 20-22 for me – they've been out shopping for days, but the clothes are horrible. Some things are so flowery and shapeless. There are loads of funky clothes out there in larger sizes.

## Sam Nixon

**Age: 17**
**From: Barnsley**

### What were you like at school?

I was head boy. I was well-behaved, really. I didn't have to do that much, it was just a funky badge to put on my tie. Did I have many girlfriends? No!

### First song written:

With Fareview; we started as a school band playing the summer and Christmas concerts. The song were called 'What You Mean To Me'; the lyrics were 'When I wake up in the morning/And I see the sparkle in your eyes/And I know what you mean to me.' I were 12 when I wrote it.

Simon came to the house and played you the song the winner will record as a single… He was really excited. Then he went on TV the next day and said we were so nice he wanted all of us to win. He knows how to pick songs. He said he wanted it to be cooler this year, and get the right song for that very moment. It's got to connect with people. I think he had a cup of Ribena while he was here. He's a nice bloke.

**How do you feel, now you know you could win?**

I'm trying to get my head round it. It's weird. We all know we're in with a chance. But I don't think about being the winner – it seems strange. And then on Saturday we find out the final two … *very* strange.

**What's been the best advice you've been given during the show's run?**

To enjoy it. And that it's about everything, not just singing – it's performing as well.

**Have you changed since your first audition?**

I have changed. I feel like I can look after myself now. I could live by myself. I thought I'd be some homebird. I love my family to bits, but I know I can be independent now.

**Who do you think should win?**

I can't say, both deserve to win. I get on with them both so well. Mark and I met at the Criterion and sang Uptown Girl together - we bonded then.

**What's been the highlight of the show for you?**

The fact that I've got this far. With the wildcard show, I were given a second chance, I'm so grateful and I've done well.

**Have you had a tantrum yet?**

No, not really. Last Saturday we all got emotional when Chris went, but no diva strops!

# Mark Rhodes

*Age:* 22
*From: Darleston, West Midlands*

**What were you like at school?**

My attendance record left a lot to be desired. Some lessons I turned up to, but RE was pants, and I didn't like science. Actually, I only liked PE and English; but I missed school quite a lot because I was diagnosed with ulcerative colitus, which saps your energy. But I was never a bad child.

**First song written:**

I was in a band at school called Clifton, which is the name of a Bingo hall near me. We did all our own songs. One of the songs was 'Take Me', which was about not taking drugs. None of my friends saw the point of taking them. We had another song called '' 'Superstar', the chorus went: 'I'm a superstar/ Drive a flash car/ And it's all right.'

**Worst thing about school:**

I had a few fights, over girls mainly. Then one lad took a real dislike to me, he was a big guy, massive. I had to take him on. When you get punched in the face you have to. I didn't win.

**How do you feel, now you know you could win?**

I love the fact I'm not expected to go through this week. There's no pressure on me at all, unlike Sam who everyone says will win, I don't think I could cope with that. The only reason I made it to the Criterion was that I made the judges laugh [he made a cheeky chappie comment to each one]. Every time I see the footage I cringe, but if I hadn't done it I wouldn't be here.

**What's been the best advice you've been given during the show's run?**

Keep your feet on the ground, my dad told me that. Your family are the most important thing. You can't get caught up in the bubble of success.

**Who do you think should win?**

I don't care, 'cos I want to win! No, I couldn't pick.

**What's been the highlight of the show for you?**

The two times the judges all agreed I would go out. I always look at Simon and give him a huge grin.

**Have you had a tantrum yet?**

I did, at the video shoot for the single. I got really narked. There was always someone looking for me …even if I was only going to the loo!

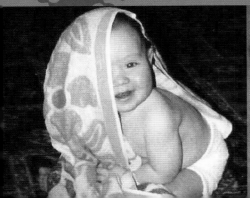

Wednesday in the *Pop Idol* mansion and everyone's keeping a low profile. The remaining three shot the video for the winner's single yesterday – they got up at 5am and got home at 10.30pm. Only Michelle is up, having a cup of tea in the kitchen. The boys are still asleep upstairs. All three slept in the same bedroom last night for the first time, but when the boys do get up, they're complaining.

'It's Michelle's snoring,' says Mark. 'And it's not just when she breathes out, it's when she breathes in.'

Michelle is moving back to her bedroom upstairs. 'I know I snore,' she admits, munching a bacon sarnie. 'Sorry for keeping you up.'

'Eh, and where's my sarnie?' asks Mark.

'I make you loads of food!' counters Michelle. Ah, they're bickering. Readers, they're like family.

While Sam does his washing in the basement, a new addition to the house is being delivered: a 'cinema bed'. It costs £15,000; you can play DVDs on it and it makes toast. Well, it doesn't quite do that, but it is very James Bond. It arrives in pieces, and is assembled in the boys' bedroom and everyone wants a go on it. But not in a pervy way, people.

This week, despite the bed, the contestants are philosophical. They know they've got this far; they know they're closer to winning it but someone still has to go on Saturday. Them's the rules of the game.

When Simon told Mark last week that 'at least he'd have time to do his Christmas shopping', the nation gasped. How rude, they thought. Even Pete Waterman said it was 'the cruellest thing ever said on British television.' And then Mark stayed – 'he is Tigger, he keeps bouncing back,' says Nicki. But will he wreak his revenge on Saturday? Mark says it takes the pressure off him, knowing he could go. But does it really? We'll have to see.

The other two are determined. They've got to sing better than before. Sam admits last week the nerves really got to him, 'And it doesn't make you perform as good. I'm normally OK, not too unconfident.'

This week, not only have they recorded the song, the video and gone busking (winner: Michelle with over £14; a little Dutch courage for herself and Mark beforehand, mind),

they've sung at Wembley. Yes, Wembley Stadium, in front of thousands of screaming fans. They met Gareth Gates and Liberty X. 'Gareth was incredible,' says Michelle. 'He just lit up the stage when he went on.' They all adored the experience, but are upset to see a Teletext review the next day, as they are lounging in their living room. Sam is praised, as is Mark, but Michelle is described as 'unremarkable' and her voice 'not powerful enough'. Michelle gets grumpy for a moment, then decides to forget about it. Very grounded, that girl.

Back to the show, and the three have decided to have fun with it. But when it's showtime, the nerves loom again like gloomy shadows and, if the *Official Pop Idol Book* can be honest, each contestant has a real problem belting out the songs. Sam gets two rockier numbers to sing, Michelle has R&B and a big ballad and Mark gets pop and soul. They have a go, but nobody really pushes it to the so-called 'next level.'

| | **Best comment** | **Worst comment** |
|---|---|---|
| **Sam** | Foxy: *'All you have to think about is who is joining you next week.'* | Simon: *'Your weakest performance so far.'* |
| **Michelle** | Simon: *'I can't imagine the the final without you.'* | Nicki: *'You sang through your nose, you have to conquer that.'* |
| **Mark** | Pete: *'That was two great songs and you did very well.'* | Foxy: *'Far too cabaret for my liking.'* |

The judges, like the contestants, are also philosophical after the show. When Foxy says he didn't see anyone thinking 'I can win this', Pete agrees. 'I thought it was flat,' says Waterman. 'But no professional has to get up and sing in front of millions of viewers every week and it's a daunting task.'

'But it's not an impossible task we gave them,' says Simon, Simonly. Mark, too, is thoughtful. 'Nerves played a part with all of us,' he says. 'We're all so hungry for it now,' says Michelle, keenly. They all look a bit sick. Perhaps nerves kicked again because they knew James Hewitt was in the audience. (He loved it, by the way, hasn't got a favourite and no, he is saving his telephone vote for the final.)

Darius is also in the building, singing a track from his forthcoming album and wishing our three buddies all the luck in the world. This was the week he went out, so it's all a bit bizarre, but testament to the fact that although he didn't win he's done really well and has pots o' cash.

Now come the results. Those awful, rubbish, horrific, terrifying but completely compelling what-a-good-TV-show-this-is results. Two judges predict Mark. (You'd think they'd have learnt by now.) Michelle is mentioned but Simon says he doesn't have a clue this week. There's only 4% between the bottom two percentages.

And the one going out this week is … Sam! The bookies' favourite! Big gasps all round and that funereal feeling starts up again as everyone asks 'Why?' and decides that yes, again, the nation has gone completely loopy.

'I'm gutted,' says Sam – who does not shed a tear but leaves Mark and Michelle to blub. 'I can't believe it!' says Michelle. And she can't. Darius says he's shocked – oh, everyone does. Because we all are, every last one of us. Pete is now more assured than ever that the show is 'not about the music anymore.'

Sam still looks composed. 'I'm feeling surprisingly good about myself,' he says. 'Good luck to both the others. I love them to bits.' The only thing he doesn't want to do is go to college next week, and he won't, because he'll have to court the press and media. Yus.

Nicki Chapman is on hand to tell Sam not to worry, because he's brill. 'He does have a passion for music and a unique voice. I'm sure the future will be rosy.'

*What they sang:…*

| | |
|---|---|
| **Michelle** | *'Say A Little Prayer'* (Diana Ross) *'Without You'* (Nilsson) |
| **Mark** | *'Back For Good'* (Take That) *'If You Don't Know Me By Now'* (Simply Red) |
| **Sam** | *'Maggie May'* (Rod Stewart) *'Always'* (Bon Jovi) |

**73**

## Nicki Chapman

**OK, so who do you think will win?**
I thought it was going to be between Sam and Michelle.

**Could you have predicted the last three?**
No. I would have never have put Mark in the last three. I thought Roxanne would have least got into the four, and I thought Andy would have been in the five.

**What sort of advice do they ask for when they're voted out?**
They very rarely ask for advice, because their emotions are all over the place. They're not thinking long-term. I think realistically, for most of them, it's the end of the road. As hard as that is, that's the truth. *Pop Idol* can only spawn so many success stories.

**What's the best rumour you've heard about the yourself?**
The best one was that I started to undress in front of one the contestants – one of the boys. *Hello*? I don't think so. I read that Susanne had to have bodyguards, and that's certainly not true.

**If two contestants really hated each other, would you reveal it on TV?**
No, because we're not doing a fly-on-the-wall show. There's a big difference. This isn't *Big Brother*.

**Out of all four judges you seem to have the most contact with the contestants...**
Last year I got to know them one on one; this year I decided not to. I think it would be very hard to give any judgement if you were friendly with them and on Saturday I went, 'That was dreadful.'

**Do you keep your ear to the ground for gossip about contestants – who's stroppy etc.?**
I tend not to read stuff on them in the papers. I'm not interested. But if the production crew told me something… well, there was the Rik Waller situation last series. I think we were all very respectful last year and that was a mistake. We should have said what we thought. I think I'd be sued if I say what I really think about him now. If I saw that kind of behaviour again I would say, 'That was a great performance but I think off-camera your personality sucks.'

**There have been lots of rumours in the press about contestants already being promised deals ...**
Simon Fuller [head of 19] won't make any decision on anybody until the competition is over. This competition is about one person, that's the winner.

**What advice do you have for the winner?**
Because you win a competition, you don't know everything. Keep your options open and listen to good advice.

# Simon Cowell

**OK, so who do you think will win?**
Erm, well I've always said Michelle, so I'll stick by it.

**Could you have predicted the last two?**
No. It would have been an interesting final to see Sam and Michelle, but this guy Mark – you can't take it away from him. He's up there and maybe he is the ultimate dark horse. We'll see.

**Were you surprised on Saturday?**
I was. I said on the night, Sam certainly wasn't his best. The whole show, to be honest with you, was uninspiring.

**You and Pete have a way of looking bored, when you're unimpressed you show it.**
I'm glad actually. It's supposed to be a reality show. When we do get bored, we *should* show it.

**What on earth are the Public playing at?**
They're voting for their favourites. I don't think anything tactical or weird is going on.

**What's been the over-riding thing that people have said to you when they've stopped you on the street?**
Most people are happy we've got someone like Michelle in the competition, who doesn't conform to the norm.

**Why is the song choice so important on the show?**
Part of the fun of *Pop Idol* is during the competition itself, watching them get it right and wrong. If it was perfect I don't think it would be fun to watch. Ironically, I think the Judges Choice is something we should never do again.

**Do you take your role as a judge seriously?**
Listen, I'm not a politician, governing the country. It's part of my job. I'm employed as a so-called expert. It's part of the fun of the show.

**What advice do you have for the winner?**
Don't believe the hype. And work hard.

**'Simon Cowell should be in charge of Iraq' said one 16 year old in the newspaper.**
I don't know about that, but I think what she was trying to respond to was the fact that I do continually try and tell the truth. I think people are fed up with being spun.

**Have you met the Prime Minister, then, to discuss this?**
Yes, I met Tony Blair, and we may be doing something about that next year. The first thing I asked him was why his politicians wasted time debating that silly issue in the House of Commons when they raised the motion we were discriminating against overweight kids. The irony was that we were supporting people like that on the show.

**What have you learnt from the Pop Idol experience about how to deal with the winner and create a consistent artist?**
It's very difficult to say what the lesson is. You get what you get. We asked for individuals. We got them. You have to take each one as they come.

# Foxy

**OK, so who do you think will win?**
[Long pause.] Michelle. But I think it's going to be a very close final. I was surprised on Saturday and – I wasn't crying – but it was the first time in this series that I felt upset by the result. I think we've been left with quite a lacklustre final, personally.

**Could you have predicted the last two?**
No, I thought Sam going through to the final was an inevitability.

**What on earth are the Public playing at?**
They're voting for underdogs all the time. I think people thought Sam would be safe. He was way above the other two. But I chose 'Back For Good' for Mark and it worked.

**You haven't had much contact with the contestants...**
Not at all during the week. I think Kate Thornton gets close to them. She spends so much time with them, she's bound to get emotionally involved. I just want to do what the public do and watch them on Saturday. That's why we don't go to rehearsals anymore. We watch it, and judge what we see.

**Do you keep your ear to the ground for gossip about contestants – who's stroppy etc.?**
These are very young kids, and they're being asked questions by some very clever journalists. They're not all going to get on. I know there was some tension in that house, but I will just judge people on what I see. Pete and I are the lucky ones – we have no vested interest in who wins. Whereas Simon and Nicki do. If they hear that someone is already a prima donna and slagging everyone off, they're thinking, 'If you win, will you be difficult?'

**What's been the over-riding thing that people have said to you when they've stopped you on the street?**
They've said, 'There's no Will.' We're lacking the x-factor we had last year. We have got a different bunch this time. *But* people are saying that as a TV show they think it's even better than last year.

**What advice do you have for the winner?**
Enjoy the ride. It will be an amazing. Their lives have changed already, but whoever wins, their life will change *immeasurably*.

**What's the best rumour you've heard about the show/yourself?**
That we're all really jealous and sick to death of Simon's success in America. I'm overjoyed for him. He's an old friend and I'm very happy he's done it.

**What's been the highlight?**
People saying they enjoy this series more than the first. A lot of people thought we couldn't do it again and it's been nice proving this wasn't a one-hit wonder.

# Pete Waterman

**OK, so who do you think will win?**

I haven't got a clue. It's changed so much over the last five weeks. The public are not voting for singers; so they must be voting for personalities. But then there are no great personalities left in. Michelle *has not* got a larger-than-life personality. Mark has a charming, West Midlands attitude to life, but is that enough to win £4 million worth of prize? Doesn't sound a good deal to me.

**Could you have predicted the last three?**

No. I love Mark 'cos he's from Walsall, but I can't see how he got in the top five. I'd have put Roxanne and Andy up there, but when they went out, I lost the plot.

**Do the contestants differ this time around?**

It's a different show this year. I think it's more karaoke, which was inevitable because we put too many people through who weren't necessarily great singers. I do sit there like a lemon sometimes, wondering why they've got me, a *musical* judge.

**Was it wise to say you were going to bet £1 million Michelle would disappear in a year?**

Hang on a minute – it's called *humour*, which certain judges seem to have lost. This is called a TV entertainment show – *light*, a piece of frippery.

**Do you keep your ear to the ground for gossip about contestants – who's stroppy etc.?**

No. In fact, the opposite. Some of the negativity in the papers, around Susanne for instance, was very unfair. If they're cocky and arrogant the public will see that. Leaking stories is a bit out of order.

**How seriously do you take your role as judge?**

I take it very seriously, which is why I get fed up of hearing myself attacking Michelle. But I can't not. I don't understand why the other judges are suddenly going, 'Michelle is wonderful.' She's not changed since the minute I first saw her in Glasgow.

**What's been the over-riding thing that people have said to you when they've stopped you on the street?**

The honesty of this series. My complaints during the first six programmes were: stop treating it as a television show; they've got to be able to sing. Simon Cowell said the Christmas show was the best ever in the series. If it was, then I'll show my arse in Burton's window. The week before was a sensational show with Big Band, and the Christmas show was karaoke Christmas songs … Please!

**What advice do you have for the winner?**

Grab the money while you can. Simon's just had the number one single and album with Will Young, which is sensational. That proves we picked the right guy.

**What's the best rumour you've heard about the show/yourself?**

I love all the rumours that I'm going to judge *American Idol* … I find all that entertaining. I love it when people tell me what I'm doing next year.

# The Grand Final

What a week it's been. On *Pop Idol*, unlike other TV shows, you dont have to just turn and sing; you don't have to sit in a house and be filmed eating your porridge, nor do you have to go to the jungle. *Pop Idol* makes you work hard for that glittering prize. The last few days have seen Mark and Michelle trot nationwide, canvassing votes in their tour buses.

Each bus is worth £250,000, has leather interiors, DVD players, beds, kitchen etc – and Mark and Michelle both have two burly minders. The last people to tour in the bus were indie band The Black Rebel Motorcycle Club, but they haven't made it smell too much. The crowds go mental when they see the Pop Idols.

'I don't think Mark and I really understood the public support that we had,' says Michelle. 'We've been in captivity, if you like, and now we've been set free. Last time we were out and about we were no one, and this week were Pop Idols.'

'The best thing for us was getting the chance to meet people who'd been voting for us,' says Mark. 'A woman ran up to me and said she'd voted for me fifty times. Now what makes someone pick up the phone and vote for someone they don't know?' *Pop Idol*, the biggest programme on the telly, that's what.

They're both excited about the single, 'All This Time'. Michelle thinks 'both versions are really good' but totally different. They love the fact they can sing a song no one else has sung before. This week, they sing another new song and an old favourite. Mark has picked 'She's Like The Wind'. Michelle remembers when she first watched Mark sing it on telly, when she was back in Glasgow.

'It was amazing. I almost dropped my glass of wine,' she says. 'And that doesn't happen very often.' She knows the competition is going to be tough. She's picked 'On The Radio' from the infamous disco week as her repeat performance. 'When I went up to Glasgow this week, they were all shouting, "Sing "On The Radio"'! So I'm glad I picked it now.'

But of course, what's a week in *Pop Idol* when there hasn't been any controversy? Foxy and Pete have been in the papers, talking of the 'freaks and geeks' on the show. They've both been bemoaning the fact that the show 'isn't about the music anymore'. Mark had his say and told them he's been voted into the final and that was that. These two are used to the 'news'papers and try not to let their elaborate stories get to them.
Meatloaf, the singer, has also had a pop at Michelle during a live concert this week. 'The tabloids stirred it up,' says Michelle. 'Someone asked me if I thought I looked like him, and of course I don't. I'm not a man for starters. But why would he even care anyway??' Well indeed – it's a mystery to us all.

The final two look mighty laid back during Friday's rehearsal. 'Im confident about all three songs this week,' says Michelle in the canteen. 'I'm not nervous about anything. Mark and I are going to go out and have an absolute blast. We know were both winners at the end of the day.'

Mark admits, well, he is slightly nervous. And when that happens he drinks 'lots of water and I have a shot of brandy as well.' Ah. Both think they will not be able to sleep tonight. They're going back to the mansion to watch DVDs and talk, presumably, about impending fame. The polls are showing that Mark and Michelle are neck and neck in popularity at the moment. Ooh.

Saturday afternoon and the dress rehearsal has just finished. What's funny is that every bit of the show has to be done, so Mark 'won' the competition in the first rehearsal, and Michelle in the second. Post-modernists will be pleased. Will Young – here to sing from his album and wish the contestants luck – is sitting in the corner of the canteen having a cup of tea and chatting on his mobile. Pete Waterman has got here early, as usual, and is having his tea. The other finalists have just arrived and they're chatting frantically. *Pop Idol*'s most notorious songsters – Warren, Daniel and Hayley – have been invited to appear on the show, and they sit in their own corner. Mark and Michelle, who isn't having anything to eat because of her nerves, are in their dressing room, out of sight.

Here it is, the night everyone has been waiting for. The tears, the joy, the hopes, the fears and the free socks… It's been a million years since the first auditions, and now it's all over. Almost.

The judges are excited, they say. 'It'll be a great TV moment,' says Foxy. Even Prime Minister Tony Blair is excited. Apparently he watches every week.

But what did these judges say when the final two did their very first auditions? Mark was told he had a lack of star quality. 'I've heard it all a thousand times before,' said Pete to Michelle. But now look at them: they're in the ruddy final.

As they clamber on stage for the start of the show, the nerves have finally hit them. 'My bottles crashed!' says Michelle. 'I was all right till I heard the crowd,' agrees Mark.

Mark's first, and he sings 'All This Time'. He looks terrified at first. The song is neatly tailored for a boy or girl to sing, and seems quite pointedly about the competition: i.e. its about waiting all your life for this one brilliant moment. Michelle's turn, and she belts it out and looks well emotional. Perhaps this is because she knows her dad has dressed as Rod Stewart tonight, including some leopard-print trousers. Mm.

Then Mark sings 'She's Like The Wind'. Ah, it's a corker. The judges tell Mark he's done great. 'Tonight will be an interesting one,' says Nicki. Pete agrees, 'You're going to give Michelle a run for her money.'

'I think I did all right. I gave it my best shot,' says Mark.

Michelle puts her all into 'On The Radio' and the crowd go ape. 'They love you here kid, and they love you at home,' says Pete.

'I'm proud of you Michelle, I really am,' says Simon.

'I do really want this now,' says Michelle. 'But whatever happens, happens.'

The calls are coming through thick and fast as Mark and Michelle run through their final songs. Mark's mum is 'nervous' but very proud of her son. Michelle's mum is also anxious, but delighted to see her daughter in the final and thinks the whole family is now as famous as the Osbournes. Both contestants look relieved they've got through it. Nerves have gone because they're given it they're all now, and they can't do it again, can they? No.

The phone lines close and there's been a record amount of votes – 10.26 million. The text votes are more than any TV show has ever had in this country, and probably the world. Cor. The two contestants stand, hand- in-hand, and wait for the result. Cue drum roll, the winner is…

**Michelle.**

She sniffs, she wipes a tear from her eye and she nearly falls backwards with shock (Mark has to steady her). 'I just wanna say thanks!' she parps. 'And for everyone who said I couldn't do it, I've done it!' Michelle's dad John is speechless, and hugs everyone. 'I apologise!' he sniffs, but he has no need.

Nicki Chapman thinks it's been an 'amazing evening, to get 10.2 million votes – its over a million more than last year. It goes to show this show has gripped the nation. They are bothered and they do want to have a say who wins.' The first bit of advice she'll give Michelle is to have 'a large drink and enjoy Christmas' because there's going to be a lot of hard work ahead. Foxy is pleased with the result too, 'I do believe Michelle should have won tonight. She was in a different league.'

Simon is very calm about the whole thing. 'It's a good result, but I'm not surprised. It was fairly obvious from her performance that she was going to win.'

And John and Ce Ce, those tireless vocal coaches who have worked with her for so very long? 'She sung like a pro,' says John. 'Im really happy for her. And so ends another chapter in *Pop Idol*….'

And, sadly, it's the last chapter in this book. 'But as one journey ends, another begins,' says Ce Ce. And she's right.

## A bit about the song:

How did Simon pick the single?
'We had a load of songs sent in. When I heard this song for the first time I liked it because I thought it was quite a cool record. I also thought lyrically it summed up what the finalist will be feeling at the time he or she has won. It wouldn't have felt right if you'd had a jolly uptempo record at the end. It's a dramatic moment, those last three minutes. My attitude is, the final three have to have fairly strong voices – at least you hope so – so you find a singer's song. We've had songs being submitted for months. But on the back of 'Evergreen' [last year's single, for those who have gone completely potty], song-writers knew what we were looking for.'

# How You Voted for Your Pop Idol 2003

**Week Seven – first live Fountain show**

| | | | |
|---|---|---|---|
| 1st | Suzanne | 16.8% | |
| 2nd | Sam | 12.4% | |
| 3rd | Chris | 11% | |
| 4th | Marc D | 11% | (by 80 votes) |
| 5th | Michelle | 9.9% | |
| 6th | Kim | 8.2% | |
| 7th | Andy | 7.1% | |
| 8th | Roxanne | 5.2% | |
| 9th | Brian | 5.2% | |
| 10th | Mark R | 4.9% | |
| 11th | Kirsty | 4.2% | (eliminated) |
| 12th | Leon | 4% | (eliminated) |

**Week Eight**

| | | | |
|---|---|---|---|
| 1st | Michelle | 17.2% | |
| 2nd | Andy | 16% | |
| 3rd | Roxanne | 13.4% | |
| 4th | Suzanne | 13.2% | |
| 5th | Sam | 11.1% | |
| 6th | Chris | 7.2% | |
| 7th | Mark R | 7.1% | |
| 8th | Kim | 5.7% | |
| 9th | Brian | 5% | (eliminated) |
| 10th | Mark D | 4.2% | (eliminated) |

**Week Nine**

| | | | |
|---|---|---|---|
| 1st | Suzanne | 22.3% | |
| 2nd | Mark R | 15.5% | |
| 3rd | Chris | 13.5% | |
| 4th | Andy | 12.3% | |
| 5th | Sam | 11.5% | |
| 6th | Michelle | 10.7% | |
| 7th | Roxanne | 9.6% | |
| 8th | Kim | 4.6% | (eliminated) |

**Week ten**

| | | | |
|---|---|---|---|
| 1st | Michelle | 23.3% | |
| 2nd | Sam | 16.8% | |
| 3rd | Roxanne | 16.5% | |
| 4th | Suzanne | 11.9% | |
| 5th | Mark R | 10.9% | |
| 6th | Chris | 10.9% | (by 697 votes) |
| 7th | Andy | 9.8% | (eliminated) |

**Week Eleven**

| | | | |
|---|---|---|---|
| 1st | Michelle | 24.3% | |
| 2nd | Sam | 18% | |
| 3rd | Chris | 16.9% | |
| 4th | Suzanne | 13.8% | |
| 5th | Mark | 13.7% | |
| 6th | Roxanne | 13.2% | (eliminated) |

**Week Twelve**

| | | | |
|---|---|---|---|
| 1st | Sam | 34.2% | |
| 2nd | Michelle | 29% | |
| 3rd | Mark | 15.1% | |
| 4th | Chris | 12.2% | |
| 5th | Suzanne | 9.7% | (eliminated) |

**Week Thirteen**

| | | | |
|---|---|---|---|
| 1st | Michelle | 40% | |
| 2nd | Sam | 23.4% | |
| 3rd | Mark | 19% | |
| 4th | Chris | 17.5% | (eliminated) |

**Week Fourteen**

| | | | |
|---|---|---|---|
| 1st | Michelle | 40.3% | |
| 2nd | Mark | 33.6% | |
| 3rd | Sam | 26% | (eliminated) |

**Week Fifteen**

| | | |
|---|---|---|
| Michelle: | 58.2% | |
| Mark: | 41.8% | |

## What they sang:

**Mark**
'All This Time'
'She's Like The Wind'
(Patrick Swayze)
'Measure Of A Man'

**Michelle**
'All This Time',
'On The Radio'
(Donna Summer)
'The Meaning Of Love...'
and then
'All This Time' again,
because she's won ...